ADVANCE PRAISE FOR MASTERING DIGITAL BU

'Nicholas Evans is a magician, weaving together the complexities of the digital worla ino a tapestry of opportunities for alert companies and managers. And like a good magician, he makes it look easy. Get started on your digital transformation with this book NOW.'
Henry Chesbrough, professor at UC Berkeley Haas School of Business, and author, Open Innovation: The New Imperative for Creating and Profiting from Technology

'The digital transformation, based on vast data from cheap sensors and cloud intelligence, will enable new business models, new strategies, and new empires in all industries. Using insight and case studies, Mastering Digital Business does a superb job guiding us through the changes coming, and helping us think through not only new product and logistics strategies, but how management itself must evolve to thrive in the coming decades.'
R. Preston McAfee, Chief Economist, Microsoft

'By their very nature, transformations require disruptive changes. Digital transformations require companies to be in a state of constant change. Mastering Digital Business shows that successful digital transformation goes beyond leading edge technology to include disruptive business models, redesigned processes, and – most importantly – cultural change.'
Jonathan Becher, Chief Digital Officer, SAP

'Mastering Digital Businesses is a highly topical book and a must read for both business and IT executives looking to come out on top by leveraging disruptive technologies. Nick is a brilliant writer and in this book he combines case studies with in-depth analysis to provide valuable insights for digital leaders. The importance for traditional players to swiftly move towards a more agile and flexible digital environment while blending the "new" with the "old" can't be understated and Nick takes the reader through a straightforward thought process for how to do this successfully.'
Robert Eriksson, Head of Engineering, Digital and Transformation, Lloyds Banking Group

'Much talk is happening about digital transformation and innovation. Rarely does this talk cover pragmatic steps regarding how to "make sense" and "take action" on the new opportunities that today's most disruptive technologies catalyze. Nick's book does that – providing "blueprints for action" – helping those who take advantage of Nick's insights move from conceptual discussions to pragmatic action, with speed and scale. Of particular value is his distillation of patterns – or what he calls "palette" – of options of which technologies to use in which combination to take advantage of different business opportunities.'
Ralph Welborn, CEO, Imaginatik

'With 52% of the Fortune 500, merged, acquired, gone bankrupt, or fallen off the list since 2000, the digital revolution has transformed business models. Leaders need pragmatic advice from strategy to execution on digital transformation. Nicholas' book Mastering Digital Business provides practitioners with not only the first principles required to succeed but also a pragmatic approach to addressing the change management requirement for success in decoding digital business.'
R. "Ray" Wang, Principal Analyst and Founder, Constellation Research

MASTERING DIGITAL BUSINESS

BCS, THE CHARTERED INSTITUTE FOR IT

BCS, The Chartered Institute for IT champions the global IT profession and the interests of individuals engaged in that profession for the benefit of all. We promote wider social and economic progress through the advancement of information technology, science and practice. We bring together industry, academics, practitioners and government to share knowledge, promote new thinking, inform the design of new curricula, shape public policy and inform the public.

Our vision is to be a world-class organisation for IT. Our 70,000 strong membership includes practitioners, businesses, academics and students in the UK and internationally. We deliver a range of professional development tools for practitioners and employees. A leading IT qualification body, we offer a range of widely recognised qualifications.

Further Information
BCS, The Chartered Institute for IT,
First Floor, Block D,
North Star House, North Star Avenue,
Swindon, SN2 1FA, United Kingdom.
T +44 (0) 1793 417 424
F +44 (0) 1793 417 444
www.bcs.org/contact

http://shop.bcs.org/

MASTERING DIGITAL BUSINESS
How powerful combinations
of disruptive technologies are
enabling the next wave of digital
transformation

Nicholas D. Evans

Published by BCS Learning & Development Ltd, a wholly owned subsidiary of BCS, The Chartered Institute for IT, First Floor, Block D, North Star House, North Star Avenue, Swindon, SN2 1FA, UK.
www.bcs.org

ISBN: 978-1-78017-345-0
Hardback ISBN: 978-1-78017-362-7
PDF ISBN: 978-1-78017-346-7
ePUB ISBN: 978-1-78017-347-4
Kindle ISBN: 978-1-78017-348-1

Ebook available

British Cataloguing in Publication Data.
A CIP catalogue record for this book is available at the British Library.

Disclaimer:
The views expressed in this book are of the author and do not necessarily reflect the views of the Institute or BCS Learning & Development Ltd except where explicitly stated as such. Although every care has been taken by the author and BCS Learning & Development Ltd in the preparation of the publication, no warranty is given by the author or BCS Learning & Development Ltd as publisher as to the accuracy or complete-ness of the information contained within it and neither the author nor BCS Learning & Development Ltd shall be responsible or liable for any loss or damage whatsoever arising by virtue of such information or any instructions or advice contained within this publication or by any of the aforementioned.

BCS books are available at special quantity discounts to use as premiums and sale promotions, or for use in corporate training programmes. Please visit our Contact us page at www.bcs.org/contact

Typeset by Lapiz Digital Services, Chennai, India.

Cover image and case study image printed with the kind permission of Mercedes AMG Petronas Formula One.

To my wife, Martha

CONTENTS

LIST OF FIGURES

LIST OF TABLES

AUTHOR

NICHOLAS D. EVANS is a Vice President and General Manager within the Office of the Chief Technology Officer at Unisys. One of *Consulting Magazine*'s 'Top 25 Consultants', and one of *ComputerWorld*'s Premier 100 IT Leaders, he leads the Applied Innovation program for the company, an internal and client-facing worldwide initiative.

Mr Evans leads Portfolio Innovation for the corporate-wide portfolio of service offerings and oversees global strategy and thought leadership with respect to the company's focus on digital transformation – as well as disruptive technologies and trends including social, mobile, analytics, cloud, IoT, intelligent automation and cyber security.

Mr Evans has over 25 years of consulting experience in all aspects of practice leadership and solution delivery in a wide variety of industries. He is the author of several books on digital business including titles from the BCS (*Mastering Digital Business*), Financial Times/Prentice Hall (*Business innovation and disruptive technology: harnessing the power of breakthrough technology...for competitive advantage* and *business agility: strategies for gaining competitive advantage through mobile business solutions*), Microsoft Press and Powersoft Press.

He has shared his perspectives in leading publications such as *Fortune*, *Time Magazine*, the *Financial Times*, *CIO Magazine*, *Computerworld*, *Optimize*, *Internet Week*, *RFID Journal* and *Washington Technology*, as well as broadcast media such as CNBC Squawk Box, Discovery Channel and The History Channel.

Prior to Unisys, Mr Evans was Global Consulting Practice Leader, Emerging Technology at BearingPoint, Inc. (formerly KPMG Consulting). In this role, he focused on the delivery of emerging technology strategies and solutions, including IoT/RFID, wireless/mobility, web services, business process management, real-time infrastructure and security, having strategic enterprise value to BearingPoint clients.

Prior to BearingPoint, Mr Evans was the National Technical Director for E-Business at PricewaterhouseCoopers. He co-founded the National Internet Consulting Practice for Coopers & Lybrand in 1997.

Mr Evans holds a BSc (Hons) in Geophysical Sciences and an MSc in Oceanography from Southampton University, UK which is ranked among the top 1% of universities worldwide. A Fellow of BCS The Chartered Institute for IT, he serves as a frequent advisor to the venture capital community and has served on numerous boards. His extracurricular interests include triathlon, having been a member of Team USA in 2010–11 and US National Champion in the Sprint Distance in his division in 2011.

He can be reached at ndevans@hotmail.com, @NicholasDEvans, or www.linkedin.com/in/nicholasdevans.

ACKNOWLEDGEMENTS

First, I'd like to thank BCS, for their generous interest, willingness and enthusiasm to take on this project. In particular, I'd like to thank Ian Borthwick, Martin Cooper, Jemma Davis-Smith, Florence Leroy, Amanda Matheson, Brian Runciman and Becky Youe for all their outstanding help and advice along the journey from initial proposal to final product. Thanks also to Denise Bannerman at Bannerman Editorial Services, and Karen Greening at Sunrise Setting Ltd in Brixham, Devon. I'd also like to thank my agent, John Willig, for his patience and advice every step of the way and for always believing in the work.

To all the executives, leaders, visionaries and subject matter experts with whom I've had the opportunity to exchange ideas and gain insights, and even in-depth case studies, thank you for your time and your willingness to collaborate and share your world-class capabilities and successes.

In particular, a big 'thank you' to all my colleagues at Unisys, Tom Reilly with Cloudera, David Sanders with Dallas Advisory Partners, Ralph Welborn with Imaginatik, Steve Hill with KPMG, Ben Cowley and Matt Harris with the Mercedes AMG Petronas Formula One Team, and Stephen Foreshew-Cain with the UK Government Digital Service. Thanks also go to Peter C. Evans with the Center for Digital Enterprise, Stephen Mellor with the Industrial Internet Consortium, Jonathan Crane with IPsoft, Adriaan den Heijer with Air France-KLM, Jim Lawton with Rethink Robotics and Steve Cousins with Savioke. Your perspectives, experience and expertise are truly appreciated and I hope I've done justice to our fascinating conversations within the scope of this book.

To my editors at *Computerworld*, including Melissa Andersen, Joyce Carpenter, Jamie Eckle and Rebecca Linke, thank you for the opportunity to contribute to your outstanding publication and for granting me a platform to share my opinions on managing innovation and disruptive technology with the global technology community.

Finally, I'd like to thank my family for your patience as always as I worked on the material over the course of several months in 2016.

ABBREVIATIONS

5D	five dimensional
AI	Artificial intelligence
API	Application programming interface
AR	Augmented reality
B2B	Business to business
B2C	Business to consumer
BWV	Body worn video
CDO	Chief digital officer
CEO	Chief executive officer
CIO	Chief information officer
CMO	Chief marketing officer
CPS	Cyber-physical production systems
CTO	Chief technology officer
DCX	Digital customer experience
EDH	Enterprise data hub
FTE	Full-time employee
GDP	Gross domestic product
GDS	Government Digital Service
GDSS	Group decision support software
GPS	Global Positioning System
HD	High definition
IaaS	Infrastructure as-a-service
ICT	Information and communications technology
IDS	Intrusion detection system
IoT	Internet of Things

IP	Intellectual property
ITSM	IT service management
MPS	Metropolitan Police Service
NFC	Near field communication
OBD	On-board diagnostics
PaaS	Platform as-a-service
R&D	Research and development
RFID	Radio frequency identification
ROI	Return on investment
SaaS	Software as-a-service
SDDC	Software-defined data centre
SDN	Software-defined network
SMAC	Social, mobile, analytics and cloud
SME	Subject matter expert
SIAM	Service integration and management
SOA	Service oriented architecture
UAV	Unmanned aerial vehicle

INTRODUCTION

Today, chief executive officers (CEOs) worldwide are applying digital transformation to re-think and re-design their traditional, existing business models and processes in the context of new disruptive technologies, digitally savvy consumers, ubiquitous computing and our globally connected society. This notion of digitisation is now affecting all aspects of business operations from innovation within and around actual products and services, to customer engagement, to the digital workplace, to business models and processes – and no industry is exempt.

The goal of this book is to provide a strategic guide for business and IT executives, applying today's most disruptive technologies (including social, mobile, analytics and cloud (SMAC) technologies, plus wearables, intelligent automation, robotics and the Internet of Things) in powerful combinations, together with platform business models, a mastery of digital services and leading practices in corporate innovation, to help you develop and execute your digital strategies for competitive advantage.

The issue for business and IT executives is that 'digital disruption' is here, and is impacting all industries. The challenge is how will you respond – both today and tomorrow?

The **big idea** is that the book introduces a **reference model and blueprint for decoding how leading players – including Uber and many others – have launched new digital disruptions within their target markets** by applying eight powerful combinations of disruptive technology underpinned by the power of the platform and a mastery of digital services.

It then shows how to apply the model towards **four key transformational business objectives:** enhancing the digital customer experience, transforming the digital workplace, gaining insights from analytics, and optimizing digital infrastructure and simplifying management – with a futuristic vision for each.

MASTERING DIGITAL BUSINESS =

      Function of (Disruptive Technologies + Platform Business Models + Digital Services Mastery)

      Accelerated by (Leading Practices in Corporate Innovation)

THE BUSINESS NEED

The book aims to provide a fresh, new approach to digital business strategy and execution, which describes how the next wave of emerging and disruptive technologies can be applied in *powerful combinations* to establish an agile new platform ecosystem for digital business.

This new platform enables organisations to create a highly virtualised, highly distributed, ecosystem of on-demand services providing a palette of options for specific digital business outcomes. Organisations can select the appropriate sub-set of building blocks, in the form of disruptive technologies, based on their target business outcomes.

While many books on 'digital business' focus solely on the digital customer experience, this book aims to provide a more in-depth, well-rounded picture with strategies and techniques for how to re-think and re-design business models and processes, how to transform the digital workplace by 'instrumenting the human' and 'socializing the machine', how to leverage insights from analytics to improve operational efficiencies and competitive advantage and how to apply intelligent automation to optimise infrastructure and simplify management.

The book goes beyond the commonly cited examples of tech giants such as Amazon, Netflix and Uber, and beyond the commonly cited business scenarios for each disruptive technology, to explore and unlock powerful new forms of business value in the years ahead. It provides a reference model for decoding how leading players have launched new digital disruptions within their target markets at the industry level, business model level and process level by applying powerful combinations of disruptive technology – with clear examples of each. In addition, it provides an actionable roadmap in terms of how to time your move, based on technology maturity, and how to take an agile journey to the future platform for digital business.

Another unique aspect of the book is that it explores how leaders can utilise the latest corporate innovation techniques to spur collaboration and prioritise opportunities based on business impact and ease of implementation. It shows precisely how existing corporate innovation programmes can be adapted and fine-tuned to most effectively support digital transformation both now and in the years to come.

The net result is that you will have a **strategic guide for the next wave of digital transformation**, which will help you to develop and execute your digital strategies for competitive advantage using the most advanced approaches to innovation and the latest disruptive technologies where the sum is far greater than the parts.

While many have written about discrete technologies, this is the first book that truly decodes digital business at the strategy level and which shows how powerful combinations of disruptive technologies, together with platform business models and a mastery of digital services, are enabling breakthrough results.

STRUCTURE OF THIS BOOK

The book provides a four-part framework from strategy to execution with unique, new reference models and blueprints, together with industry case studies, and practical advice gained from innovation sessions and workshops conducted with hundreds of major corporations around the world and a 25-year career working for the world's foremost consulting organisations helping global clients apply the latest emerging technologies for business advantage.

The book's approach takes the reader from **insight**, by introducing the reference model and blueprint, to **planning**, by showing how to lead and organise for digital transformation, to **action**, by showing how to apply the model towards four key transformational objectives – with a vision for each – and finally to the **roadmap**, by showing how to take an agile journey to the new platform while preserving existing investments.

In this book, you'll learn strategic approaches to:

- Design your digital business strategy and vision.
- Re-think and re-design your business models and processes.
- Maximise the potential of today's disruptive technologies for digital business.
- Organise and adapt corporate innovation processes for digital transformation.
- Identify and prioritise digital transformation opportunities with innovation workshops.
- Time your move based on the three waves of disruptive technology adoption.
- Transform the digital customer experience and the digital workplace.
- Gain competitive advantage from analytics.
- Pursue an agile journey to the new platform for digital business.
- Master the digital services lifecycle and speed time-to-market.

Here's a quick summary of the book's four-part structure:

Part I: Insight – Setting your Digital Transformation Vision introduces a reference model and blueprint for decoding how leading players have launched new digital disruptions within their target markets by applying eight powerful combinations of disruptive technology, together with platform business models.

Part II: Planning – Leading and Organising for Digital Transformation shows how to lead and organise for change, including precisely how existing corporate innovation programmes can be adapted and fine-tuned to most effectively support digital transformation.

Part III: Action – Digital Transformation Strategies for Specific Target Business Outcomes shows how to apply the model towards four key transformation objectives, including enhancing the digital customer experience, transforming the digital workplace, gaining insights from analytics, and optimising digital infrastructure and simplifying management with a vision for each.

Part IV: Roadmap – Taking an Agile Journey to the New Platform Ecosystem provides an actionable roadmap in terms of how to master the digital services lifecycle and take an agile journey to the future platform for digital business while preserving existing investments.

CONVENTIONS

In terms of conventions, there are a number of techniques used in this book to help you quickly find information, examples, case studies and key takeaways. Tables are frequently used to provide key facts, definitions of terms, concise examples of business benefits and industry scenarios. Company examples and case studies are provided within the main text of each chapter, in the context of the discussion, to help illustrate the points being made. In-depth case studies, which can be considered 'feature' case studies, are labelled 'Case study' and are highlighted within a shaded text box to make them clearly visible. These are typically self-standing and can be read at any time. Key takeaways are presented at the end of each chapter to help summarise the key points and lessons learned within the chapter, and to highlight any key approaches, techniques or models that might be useful in your own planning.

TARGET AUDIENCE

The target audience for the book is business executives and leaders, in both large and mid-size organisations, wishing to **exploit disruptive technologies** together with **leading innovation management approaches** within their business for digital transformation, continual growth, profits and relevancy, and to keep ahead of the competition.

The book is particularly suited for executives and leaders – from the C-suite to managers – who need a strategic guide to help shape and inform their digital business vision and direction. This applies equally well to any leader or manager who wears a strategy 'hat' in his or her role – including line-of-business leaders in areas such as product and service development, marketing, customer service and support, supply chain and operations, as well as IT leaders – and those in dedicated strategy positions within the organisation.

The secondary audience is technology providers, start-ups, professional services companies, venture capitalists and investors, government policy makers, educational institutions and students, industry analysts and industry associations.

PART I
INSIGHT – SETTING YOUR DIGITAL TRANSFORMATION VISION

1 DESIGNING YOUR DIGITAL BUSINESS STRATEGY AND VISION

Software is eating the world.

Marc Andreessen[1]

In this chapter, we'll explore the art of the possible with regard to digital business, why it's so disruptive to traditional business models, and how to prepare for disruption in your industry. We'll also look at some industry examples, such as smart parking, where new digitally based business models can not only disrupt their target markets but can be quickly expanded into market adjacencies.

In terms of the art of the possible, due to the 'digital medium' these new business models are designed to operate in, they have the intrinsic potential to be more transformative than they would appear from the outside. By digitising a traditionally analogue business model or process, we're effectively turning it into bits and atoms and enabling an infinite variety of possibilities.

In terms of exploring why digital business is so disruptive to traditional business models and traditional notions of industry competition, we'll analyse the situation by looking at Porter's model of the five forces of industry competition and exploring how digital business is impacting each of the various forces.

Finally, in terms of how to prepare for digital disruption, we'll explore some of the signs to watch out for and how to prepare your response. By its very nature, a disruption is extremely hard to predict. Still, with careful analysis of industry trends, a keen grasp of the art of the possible and observations of recent 'seismic activity', you can get a sense of what to prepare for and how to react.

THE ART OF THE POSSIBLE: THE HIDDEN DISRUPTION OF DIGITAL BUSINESS MODELS

Digital transformation is being applied by CEOs worldwide to re-think and re-design their traditional, existing business models and processes in the context of today's disruptive technologies, the consumerisation of IT, ubiquitous low-cost computing and our globally connected society. It's my belief that many of these new, social-, mobile-, analytics- and cloud-enabled (that is, SMAC-enabled) digital business models have the intrinsic potential to be more transformative than they would first appear from the outside.

One of the interesting questions often raised in regard to digital transformation initiatives is actually how 'transformational' the initiative really is.

Does the initiative truly create transformational change to the business model, process, product or service, or is it more of an incremental value-add?

First, this is a great question to ask of all of your digital initiatives. In essence, it is a litmus test to uncover the degree of change that's anticipated, or already experienced, from deployment of your digital initiative. As the sponsor behind the initiative, or perhaps one of several stakeholders, you'll know right away from your digital strategy the degree of change you're aiming for. As you look across your portfolio of projects, it's likely that some will be closer to the 'transformational' bar and others will be deliberately more 'incremental', but still intended to yield specific forms of measurable business value.

This 'degree of transformation' discussion is very much akin to the kinds of discussions I have with customers when conducting innovation workshops. In our particular form of these workshops, we encourage innovative ideas of all kinds: from strategic, and highly disruptive, 'change the business' types of ideas all the way to more tactical, incremental ideas. The idea with these particular workshops is that all ideas, from strategic to tactical, have initial merit and should be captured. As long as they're aligned with the key focus areas of the workshop, determined ahead of time with the workshop sponsors, and are intended to add business value, then let's go ahead and capture them for subsequent discussion and prioritisation.

As a sponsor or stakeholder you likely know the degree of transformation inherent in your initiative based upon your strategy, but what about the outside industry observer, customer or partner? As highlighted earlier, it's my belief that due to the 'digital medium' these new business models are designed to operate in, they have the intrinsic potential to be more transformative than they would appear from the outside.

As discussed, by digitising a traditionally analogue business model or process, we're effectively turning it into bits and atoms and enabling an infinite variety of possibilities. The rules can be whatever you want them to be – with the market being the petri dish to determine if the new rules are viable and can lead to adoption and growth.

 CASE STUDY – STREETLINE

A smart parking example
A good example of the hidden disruption of digital business models – in terms of the hidden degree of transformational change – is smart parking. At first glance, it's just a way to find a parking spot. Wireless sensors are embedded in parking spaces to detect whether the space is occupied or not. Data from each sensor is relayed to the cloud and then real-time parking data is published via a mobile app on the smartphone, so drivers can find open parking spots and gain access to additional data and analytics.

In terms of enabling technologies for digital business, it's a great SMAC example, because it has all the elements of social, mobile, analytics and cloud. But is it really doing anything more than giving directions to drivers on their mobile device so they can find open parking spaces in the city? Surely that's just an incremental value-add, and hardly transformative. It's just going to save me a few minutes in finding a parking spot.

When you take an in-depth look at smart parking, however, you'll find some truly transformational aspects to the digital business model – what you might call some 'hidden disruptions'. First, smart parking has obvious benefits for drivers, but it also has transformational aspects for cities and also for the transportation industry as a whole.

In addition to being a $25 billion industry that's seen little innovation in decades, parking is essentially a real estate play for cities. It's typically the second or third source of revenue for the city as a whole. Any business model or process change that can improve parking revenues, reduce time spent looking for parking, reduce traffic congestion and reduce pollution can yield substantial benefits to the local city and economy.

Table 1.1 Transformational aspects of smart parking

Key facts	Benefits	Transformational aspects
• 2 billion parking spaces in the United States • 70 million hours spent looking for parking each year representing a $1B loss to the US economy • 30% of city drivers looking for parking adding 10% to average vehicle's CO_2 emissions	• Increase city revenue by 20–30% with an ROI in 1–2 years • 30% reduction in greenhouse gas emissions • 10% reduction in traffic • 2% increase in local GDP	• Extensions of the smart parking business model into smart cities, intelligent transportation networks, and connected cars • Opportunities for smart city operations and services to become highly responsive, pro-active, and even predictive based on digitally observed changes in the real-world environment

Today, according to Streetline,[2] there are approximately 2 billion parking spaces in the US. A total of 70 million hours are spent each year looking for parking, which represents a $1 billion loss to the economy. In addition, 30% of city drivers are looking for parking and this adds about 10% to the average vehicle's CO_2 emissions.

Smart parking systems enable cities to better understand parking behaviour and make policy changes that can improve conditions. This might include changes such as parking hours of operation, parking time limits or even demand-based pricing. The result is that smart parking can enable cities to increase revenue by up to 20–30% and cities can achieve a return on investment (ROI) in one to two years.

Recent case studies have shown that sales tax revenues increased by 11.9%, a 30% reduction in greenhouse gas emissions, a 10% reduction in traffic, and an increase of 2% in local GDP. Reducing traffic and parking congestion improves commerce by making cities more accessible for all involved.

In the UK, Streetline is working with major cities such as Birmingham and Manchester. The City of Birmingham, which has over 1 million residents combined with 160,000 commuters, is using Streetline wireless parking sensors and applications to see trends including hourly occupancy, occupancy by block and parking duration. Manchester City Council has collaborated with Streetline to launch the motorist guidance app Parker™ in Manchester's vibrant Northern Quarter and Chinatown areas to prevent circling and increase foot traffic to local merchants.

So today, I'd argue there's a strong business case for smart parking with transformational levels of benefit – that is, beyond single digit percentage improvements and into the 10%-plus range. When we look ahead to extensions of this business model into smart cities, intelligent transportation networks and connected cars, that's when things get even more interesting. Is smart parking really just about parking or is it about digitising and connecting the physical world to enable a wide range of new business models and associated services? That is, the start of an Internet of Things (IoT) play.

What happens when smart parking systems get integrated into an ecosystem of other IoT devices within a city, such as air quality, lighting, water pressure and even garbage cans?

The result is opportunities for smart city operations and services to become highly responsive, pro-active and even predictive based on digitally observed changes in the real-world environment. Sensors used for one purpose may also be re-tasked or multi-tasked to serve other city purposes as well. For example, smart parking sensors that include temperature sensors can be used to measure road surface temperature and pro-actively know when salt trucks or snow removal trucks should be dispatched.

What happens when smart parking systems get integrated into the connected car?

In the near future, the result may be that your digital assistant, accessible from any device including your car, can share your schedule with relevant merchants via the smart parking ecosystem so they can reserve prime parking for you a couple of minutes ahead of your scheduled arrival time. This and hundreds other personalised services that you'll access via your mobile and your connected car will make this intelligent ecosystem very 'sticky' in terms of the services provided. Early entrant service providers and merchants will build highly personalised and curated experiences for their customers, which may be hard for later entrants to unseat.

Just as Amazon digitised the book selling industry and Netflix the movie rental industry, transportation is an example of one of the next, many industry areas to go digital. When the IoT is part of this business model as well it opens up even more possibilities for hidden disruption, since we're digitising the physical world and instrumenting people, assets and infrastructure. This has the potential to radically change how people work and live, since it moves us into an era of instant digital experiences, interactions and transactions underpinned by intelligent consumption of resources.

In summary, digital business models are highly attractive because they have so many future directions they can take and the opportunity for business model and business process innovation is wide open. The potential for transformational change is particularly strong when going from a totally analogue business model to a highly digitised one.

ANALYSING THE DISRUPTION: HOW DIGITAL DISRUPTS THE FIVE FORCES OF INDUSTRY COMPETITION

Exactly why is digital business so disruptive to traditional business models and traditional notions of industry competition?

A useful way to analyse the situation is by looking at Porter's model of the five forces of industry competition and exploring how digital business is impacting each of the various forces.

In one of his landmark books, titled *Competitive strategy*,[3] Michael E. Porter describes the five forces of industry competition as the entry of new competitors, the threat of substitutes, the bargaining power of buyers, the bargaining power of suppliers, and the rivalry among existing competitors. The Five Forces Model has long been used by corporate strategists to think about the rules of competition and the respective headwinds and tailwinds produced as a company operates and produces products or services in this external environmental context.

Traditionally, strategists would develop approaches to minimise the headwinds and maximise the tailwinds associated with each force. For example, the threat of new entrants could be minimised by creating strong barriers to entry in terms of patents and other rights, large economies of scale, product differentiation, strong customer loyalty and high switching costs. As another example, the threat of substitute products or services could be minimised by creating a higher level of differentiation or better price performance when compared to competitive offerings.

Digital business is impacting each of these traditional forces and essentially levelling the playing field to the point where new entrants can rush in with far fewer barriers to entry. In fact, these new players may well have a competitive advantage over incumbents, even from day one, simply by having a digitally based business model.

In some cases, not only is digital disruption coming to various industries via the free market economy, it is also being regulated into effect. Take for example, the Revised Directive on Payment Services (PSD2) which is designed to create safer and more innovative European payments. PSD2 is having a highly disruptive effect on the financial services industry because it requires banks to open up access to customer's online accounts and payment services to third party providers. Banks are therefore being forced to re-think their business models and the very ecosystems in which they operate.

Table 1.2 provides a listing of the traditional five forces together with a summary of how the new digital threat (i.e. the threat of digital disruption) is impacting these traditional forces – creating both threats and opportunities – and the rationale for how and why digital is making such a transformational impact.

Table 1.2 New digital threats impacting the Five Forces Model

Traditional force	New digital threat	Rationale
The entry of new competitors	New entrants from outside your industry, equipped with new digitally based business models and value propositions.	• Digital business changes the rules by lowering the traditional barriers to entry. • A digitally based business model requires far less capital and can bring large economies of scale.
The threat of substitutes	Purely digital substitutes, hybrid digital/physical substitutes and digital services wrapped around a physical product.	• Switching costs are low and buyer propensity to substitute is high.
The bargaining power of buyers	Bargaining power lays out a new set of expectations for the digital customer experience and is the biggest driver of digital business.	• Instant access to information as well as insights from social media. • Price sensitivity and low switching costs via digital channels. • Access to substitute products and services with greater ease of use and convenience.
The bargaining power of suppliers	Suppliers can accelerate or slow down the adoption of a digitally based business model, based upon how it impacts their own situation.	• Use of APIs within digital ecosystems can streamline ability to form new partnerships and manage existing ones. • Bargaining power can also slow down or dispute the validity or legality of the new digital model.

(continued)

Table 1.2 (Continued)

Traditional force	New digital threat	Rationale
The rivalry among existing competitors	Entry and exit barriers are going down due to the comparative low cost of digital business models.	• New entrants do not even need to own physical assets or infrastructure. • The 'platform' model is seeing success by connecting stakeholders and providing services that enhance the customer experience.

1. The entry of new competitors

There's no doubt that digital business is changing the nature of competition. Today, it's not just traditional industry competitors you need to worry about, but new entrants from outside your industry, equipped with new digitally based business models and value propositions.

This is often tech giants and start-ups that have envisioned and built a new business model from the ground up, powered by a new platform ecosystem for digital business. They're leveraging the familiar SMAC technologies, but are often adding in personas and context, intelligent automation, the IoT and cyber security to further enhance the value proposition of their platform.

In effect, tomorrow's leader may not be someone you know. We often think of industry competition as a perpetual battle between the same set of incumbents, but in reality things are far more dynamic and transitory. As an example, whereas 89 per cent of the Fortune 500 went out of business between 1955 and 2014,[4] in recent years, according to R. 'Ray' Wang of Constellation Research, 52 per cent has been merged, acquired, gone bankrupt or fallen off the list since 2000.[5]

Why can new entrants move in so easily? Digital business changes the rules by lowering the traditional barriers to entry. A digitally based business model requires far less capital and can bring large economies of scale for example.

2. The threat of substitutes

The threat of substitutes has to do with the threat of substitute products or services. In terms of digital business, this can come from a purely digital substitute or a hybrid digital/physical substitute. Taxi services, such as Uber and EasyTaxi, for example, provide a hybrid model via a digital app for consumers and taxi drivers, coupled with the physical taxis.

Digital services wrapped around a physical product are another example and can range from one extreme such as the Industrial Internet, to another such as home automation technologies or personal fitness products. In addition, the long-term revenue stream from the digital services may be worth far more than the one-time sale of the physical product.

The threat of substitutes is high in many industries, since switching costs are low and buyer propensity to substitute is high. In the taxi services example, customers can easily switch from traditional models to the new model simply by installing an app on their smartphone.

Propensity to switch from the traditional model is high due to consumer wait times for taxis, lack of visibility into taxi location and so on.

3. The bargaining power of buyers

Perhaps the strongest of the five forces impacting industry competition is the bargaining power of buyers, since the biggest driver of digital business comes from the needs and expectations of consumers and customers themselves.

This bargaining power lays out a new set of expectations for the digital customer experience and necessitates continual corporate innovation across business models, processes, operations, products and services.

Customers and consumers have amassed far more bargaining power today due to instant access to information, insights from social media (including access to reviews and feedback), low switching costs via digital channels, price sensitivity, access to substitute products and services with greater ease of use and convenience, as well as increased industry competitiveness as a result of the other forces.

4. The bargaining power of suppliers

Suppliers can accelerate or slow down the adoption of a digitally based business model, based upon how it impacts their own situation. Those pursuing digital models themselves, such as using application programming interfaces (APIs) to streamline their ability to form new partnerships and manage existing ones, may help to accelerate your own model.

Those who are suppliers to the traditional models, and who question or are still determining their new role in the digital equivalent, may use their bargaining power to slow down or dispute the validity or legality of the new model.

Good examples are the legal and business issues surfacing around the digital-sharing economy (i.e. ride-sharing, room-sharing etc.), where suppliers and other constituents work to ensure that the business model and process innovations still adhere to established rules, regulations, privacy, security and safety. This is a positive and needed development since, coupled with bargaining power of buyers, it can help to keep new models 'honest' in terms of how they operate.

5. The rivalry among the existing competitors

Finally, existing competitors are all looking at digital business – trying to understand the disruptions occurring and prepare their response. The responses can range all the way from defensive to offensive measures, and even a first-mover attack. This rivalry among competitors is always in play, but in recent years digital business has added fuel to the fire, just as the ebusiness era did many years ago.

The rivalry is heating up because entry and exit barriers are going down due to the comparative low cost of digital business models, and in many cases new entrants do not even need to own physical assets or infrastructure. In particular, the 'platform' model is seeing considerable success in the marketplace by simply connecting stakeholders and applying a set of peripheral services to enhance the customer experience.

By doing so, platform operators are moving to the forefront of service delivery and getting closer to the customer without even owning assets or having employees working in that particular industry. According to a recent article in *The Guardian*,

> Today, any service provider, and even content provider, risks becoming hostage to the platform operator, which, by aggregating all those peripherals and stream-lining the experience of using them, suddenly moves from the periphery to the centre.[6]

Overall, as you prepare your various digital business initiatives, the five forces framework can be a useful way to think about the various headwinds and tailwinds acting on your envisioned model and how various constituents may react. In combination with the usual value chain analysis, it can help to inform your strategy and provide some useful insights into what you may encounter along the way.

PREPARING FOR THE DIGITAL DISRUPTION THAT'S COMING TO YOUR INDUSTRY

Whatever your business, significant disruption is either already occurring or on the way. Much of this is due to the latest wave of emerging and disruptive technologies that are serving as foundational building blocks for new, digitally based business models.

In talking with a number of CEOs and business leaders, all of them are keen to glimpse around the corner to prepare for what's ahead. Even if your business is going strong right now, you should be doing the same. To help you in this task, here are a few thoughts that arose from those discussions.

Understanding the disruption

By its very nature, a disruption is extremely hard to predict. Still, with careful analysis of industry trends, a keen grasp of the art of the possible, and observations of recent

---

Figure 1.1 Preparing for digital disruption

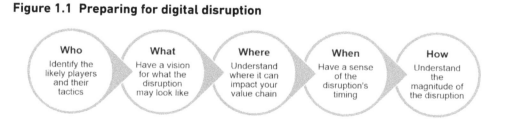

'seismic activity', you can get a sense of what to prepare for in terms of 'who', 'what', 'where', 'when' and 'how' (Figure 1.1).

1. Identify the likely players and their tactics

This is not always as easy as it sounds, since a competitor can come out of nowhere. Take as an example Apple Pay and its effect on the mobile payments industry. This was a case of a technology giant leveraging its cash flow and vast customer base and using disruptive technologies to poach on territory where it had never before set foot. Apple's limited industry knowledge was offset by its millions of customers, its eagerness to partner with major industry players to become relevant in the industry and its ability to continually turn on new services for customers.

Here's the thing, though: if you're in the payments industry, you've known for a long time that digital payments were coming. Your preparation for that day should have included the recognition that a company like Apple, with a mastery of digital services, could make a play. In Chapter 2, 'Re-thinking and re-designing your business models and processes', we'll take a more in-depth look at the digital business strategy moves behind Apple's entry into mobile payments via its Apple Pay service.

2. Understand the magnitude

A disruption can happen at the industry level, the business model level or the process level. But be aware that a process disruption can bubble up in scale and affect both business models and entire industries. Just think of what happened to travel agents when a process change (booking travel on the internet) nearly eliminated their role. We'll also explore this aspect in Chapter 2 in terms of the various pathways for re-thinking and re-designing business processes for a more agile enterprise and a transformed user experience.

3. Have a vision for what the disruption may look like

The disruption could be a technology-driven disruption such as 3D printing, or a competitive disruption in the form of new entrants with digitally based business models, processes, products or services. Within the transportation industry, for example, 3D printing is expected to threaten up to 41 per cent of air cargo and up to 37 per cent of ocean container shipments[7] as the technology starts to enable locally manufactured products and lessen the need for shipments overseas. Chapter 3, 'Maximising the potential of today's disruptive technologies for digital business', explores the various emerging and disruptive technologies that are coming together to serve as the foundational building blocks for disruptions in the form of new, digitally enabled business models, processes, products and services.

Another way to get a sense of what future disruptions may look like is to craft a vision for your industry or to look at those already under development. The German 'Industry 4.0' vision for the future of manufacturing is an example, as is GE's vision of the Industrial Internet. Chapter 4, 'The new platform ecosystem for digital business', explores how the visions of Industry 4.0 and the Industrial Internet are built upon the new platform for digital business (i.e. the foundational technology building blocks) and additionally explores the impact of digital business ecosystems and platforms, which are fast becoming the dominant go-to-market business model.

4. Have a sense of the disruption's timing

To prepare your response and time your move, it's key to estimate when these events will affect you. Is this something you need to act on immediately or something you should continue to monitor closely? Either way, it's good to have a strategic plan and weigh all the response scenarios.

Having a good sense of the timing of these disruptions is important not only to help you respond accordingly, but also to help you understand how technology maturity can enable different business opportunities. As emerging technologies are adopted in the enterprise, much like surfing, there are generally three waves you can catch along the way. A particular trend in pioneer or early adopter status needs to be handled quite differently from when it has progressed into the early majority, or even the late majority. The kinds of benefits you can expect to obtain are quite different as well.

If we take blockchain technology as an example, with blockchain (the distributed ledger technology behind Bitcoin that lets people who do not know or trust each other build a record of who owns what at any point in time) currently in the first 'emerging wave', there's strong potential for business model transformation for pioneers who are willing to take the risk. If your organisation is more conservative, you can wait for the second 'differentiating wave' to extract competitive advantage as an early adopter, or the third 'business value wave' to extract proven business value as part of the early majority. In Chapter 7, 'Timing your move based on technology maturity', we'll explore this topic in more detail so you have an in-depth understanding of the business benefits and the pros and cons of entering the market with these types of emerging technologies at different times as they mature.

5. Understand what the disruption can do to your industry's value chain

In most industries, a highly likely play will be to get closer to your customers by offering a radically different way of doing business that's faster, simpler and cheaper. In Chapter 8, 'Enhancing the digital customer experience', we'll explore some of the keys to success and the strategies around creating new, digitally based value propositions to get closer to the customer, and the importance of a seamless and compelling customer experience across all new digital processes, channels and devices.

Preparing your response

After understanding the disruption, it's time to formulate your response. Preparing your response requires strong alignment across the organisation from strategy to innovation to execution. Strategy can help to guide the innovation function in terms of strategic focus areas and help to direct innovation efforts and campaigns towards those initiatives that have the most strategic significance to customers and which are well aligned with the organisation's digital business vision, direction and capabilities.

Leading and organising for digital transformation

On the front-end, from a strategy perspective, it's important to conduct rigorous market research and put your innovation programme into overdrive. That means fine-tuning your programme across strategy and intent, people, process, technology and continuous improvement to maximise your organisational potential for digital business innovation. Chapter 5, 'Organising the adapting corporate innovation processes for digital transformation', provides leadership guidance on how to change and fine-tune an existing corporate innovation programme to most effectively support digital transformation both now and in the years to come. We also explore the five critical pillars of innovation management capability, so you can ensure that your innovation programme has all the appropriate elements for ongoing success.

In preparing your response to digital disruption, as a key element in your innovation arsenal, it's also important to conduct frequent innovation workshops and talk to customers, partners and other industry experts — even outside your industry segment. Chapter 6, 'Identifying and prioritising opportunities with innovation workshops', explores how leaders can apply these highly targeted, event-based sessions to focus on innovation opportunity identification, categorisation, prioritisation and then the development of high-level business cases and roadmaps for the most promising opportunities identified.

Digital transformation strategies for specific target business outcomes

With your innovation engine fine-tuned and ready for action, you can now begin to craft and execute your response, whether it's a defensive or offensive measure, or a first-mover attack. You might simply optimise your current position in the value chain or change your position to get closer to the customer.

One strategy for getting closer to the customer is to apply big data analytics to understand your customers' preferences, needs, interests and behaviours far better than anyone else. Collecting information about your customers' usage of your products or services may enable you to monetise the data swirling around your product or service as well, by turning it into additional value-added services for your customers.

A key factor in improved digital customer experience is re-thinking how customers do business with you, much as Uber has done for finding a taxi. This is typically where SMAC computing comes into play, but disrupters may additionally incorporate IoT business models (such as our earlier smart parking example with Streetline) or even robotics business models (as evidenced by some of the recent robotic valets appearing in hotels such as the Japanese hotel Huis Ten Bosch and the Aloft hotel chain).

Innovation can also focus on a single, yet critical, business process such as usage-based insurance models. In the insurance example, technology comes in with intelligent sensors that measure things like acceleration and hard braking, letting the insurer offer incentives for good driving behaviour – and taking loyalty programmes to the next level, with incentives based on actual driving behaviour at a highly granular level, as opposed to simply on repeat business from month to month.

If you simply want to optimise your current position in the value chain, your initial focus might be on employee-centred improvements by transforming the digital workplace or on optimisation of your IT infrastructure and operations by enabling an industrialised software-defined data centre (SDDC).

If we look more closely at enabling the digital workplace, we can see how the foundational building blocks of digitally based business models can come into play. For example, wearables such as Google Glass can enable hands-free process optimisation in areas like item picking in a warehouse. Recent trials, such as those conducted by DHL in their 'vision picking' pilots, have shown reduced error rates in the warehouse picking process and overall efficiency improvements of up to 25 per cent.[8]

Intelligent automation is another area of significant opportunity. We're already seeing the convergence of human–machine work processes, where humans are becoming increasingly instrumented and machines are becoming increasingly connected with humans to create an optimised blend of human–machine participation and interaction.

Cognitive systems and intelligent automation techniques are reducing costs and dependence on labour-based processes and optimising service efficiency. Advances in machine learning, expert systems and robotics are leading to automation opportunities in both virtual (that is, software) and physical scenarios.

A relevant software-based example is the emerging role of what are known as 'cognitive virtual agents' or 'virtual engineers' in the next-generation call centre. These agents interface on human terms in natural language. They think, speak and learn on the job – improving business processes and making better-informed decisions. A recent example is IPSoft's Amelia technology, which is being used to transform IT operations labour mix with digital labour, costing one-third of the typical human full-time employee (FTE) cost.

Chapters 8–11 take a detailed look at each of these target business outcomes around digital transformation, ranging from enhancing the digital customer experience, to transforming the digital workplace, to gaining insights from analytics and finally to optimising infrastructure and simplifying management. These areas represent some of the key value levers organisations can apply to get the most out of their digital business strategies.

Taking an agile journey to the new platform ecosystem

Going back to our value chain discussion, the business strategies and options regarding how and where to play in the future value chain are the same strategic decisions that organisations have needed to make for decades. What's new and different is the magnitude of potential business disruption and transformation via today's fresh new wave of disruptive technologies.

Your strategic response to digital disruption can make use of a rich set of foundational building blocks in the form of disruptive technologies – some mature, others emerging. Whatever your business strategy, you can select from these foundational building blocks and apply them in powerful combinations to enable your target business outcomes.

In the final chapters of this book, we'll explore how to execute your roadmap to digital transformation by mastering what it takes to manage the digital services lifecycle and in recognition that existing applications and infrastructure need to be carefully migrated or maintained.

KEY TAKEAWAYS FOR CHAPTER 1

- In terms of the art of the possible, due to the 'digital medium' new business models are designed to operate in, they have the intrinsic potential to be more transformative than they would appear from the outside.

- By digitising a traditionally analogue business model or process, we're effectively turning it into bits and atoms and enabling an infinite variety of possibilities. The rules can be whatever you want them to be – with the market being the petri dish to determine if the new rules are viable and can lead to adoption and growth.

- The five forces framework, together with our observations of how the new digital threat (that is, the threat of digital disruption) impacts these five forces, can be a useful way to think about the various headwinds and tailwinds acting on your envisioned model and how various constituents may react.

- In terms of understanding upcoming disruptions, with careful analysis of industry trends, a keen grasp of the art of the possible and observations of recent 'seismic activity', you can get a sense of what to prepare for in terms of 'who' (the likely players and their tactics), 'what' (a vision for what the disruption may look like), 'where' (where it can impact your value chain), 'when' (a sense of the disruption's timing) and 'how' (the magnitude of the disruption).

- Some of the key value levers organisations can apply to get the most out of their digital business strategies include enhancing the digital customer experience, transforming the digital workplace, gaining insights from analytics, and optimising infrastructure and simplifying management.

2 RE-THINKING AND RE-DESIGNING YOUR BUSINESS MODELS AND PROCESSES

The reason why it is so difficult for existing firms to capitalize on disruptive innovations is that their processes and their business model that make them good at the existing business actually make them bad at competing for the disruption.

Clayton Christensen[1]

Some of the most exciting opportunities for digital transformation relate to re-thinking and re-designing business models as well as re-thinking and re-designing the underlying business processes that define how these new digital business models operate, how value gets exchanged, how digital products and services are delivered, and how work gets done.

In terms of re-thinking and re-designing business models, we'll explore some of the strategic options for business model innovation, ranging from evolutionary to revolutionary approaches, and will look at how some of the classic strategy moves still apply to the world of digital. To use a chess analogy, while we're playing on a new chessboard, with new pieces and new rules, some of the traditional game sequences and strategy techniques still apply and can be highly effective. To illustrate this point, we'll take an in-depth look at the digital business strategy moves by Apple in launching and expanding their Apple Pay service for mobile payments. This was a business model innovation in the world of payments, with new players, new technology and a new approach, yet it was able to scale to become the world's leading mobile payments service with over 12 million monthly users in less than 18 months.[2]

In terms of re-thinking and re-designing business processes, we'll explore how digital business process re-design builds upon and adds to prior thinking, such as Hammer and Champy's concepts related to business process re-engineering.[3] When we examine digitally re-designed processes, we find there are a number of recurring themes and key characteristics which enable digital processes to trump traditional processes by being experience-centric, automated, simplified, digitised, personalised, dynamic, real time, granular, aggregated and scalable. To help you think further about re-design efforts within your own organisation, we'll also take an in-depth look at some of the strategic pathways for re-designing mobile business processes. These pathways are focused on improving digital–physical intensity as well as mobile technology intensity and include what we can describe as the 'wow factor', the 'must have', the 'innovative replacement' and the 'technology upgrade'.

Whether we look at transformed business models or transformed business processes, what's also clear is that the most successful initiatives all tap into the vital elements we'll continue to explore throughout this book: powerful combinations of disruptive technology enablers, platform business models and a mastery of digital services, all accelerated by leading practices in corporate innovation.

RE-THINKING AND RE-DESIGNING BUSINESS MODELS

The number of strategic options for business model innovation in the age of digital are many and varied. They range from digitising products and services, to running or participating within industry 'platforms', to tapping into the sharing economy and crowdsourcing, to reshaping value networks, to creating new models for monetisation. To help you think more about these strategic options within your own organisation, we'll look at each of these approaches to explore how they work and to provide some industry examples.

1. Digitising products and services

When we look at digitising products and services, the options range from digitising a physical product or service, to wrapping digital services around a physical product, to unbundling how digital services are provided to make them more customised and specific. Many years ago, the initial wave of business model innovation was around converting physical products such as books, music and movies to their digital equivalents. Examples include Amazon (books), Apple iTunes (music) and Netflix (movies).

Today, organisations are exploring wrapping physical products with new digital services in order to enhance their value proposition for customers. This also generates a long-term revenue stream from the digital services, which, over time, may be worth far more than the one-time sale of the physical product. Examples include GE's wrapping of data and analytics services around its core industrial products such as jet engines and gas turbines, as well as Nest's wrapping of cloud-based video recording services around its home security cameras. As another example, home fitness equipment manufacturers such as Pro-Form and NordicTrack have incorporated iFit software into their machines to provide personalised, 'smart fitness' to consumers' home training routines. With an iFit membership, users gain access to custom workouts, Google Maps™ training routes, social communities, competitions, automatic stats tracking and so on. This set of digital services integrated into the physical home fitness equipment such as treadmills, elliptical machines and bikes considerably enhances the value proposition for customers.

In terms of unbundling digital services, as an example many insurance companies are now offering far more granular insurance policies, not on a yearly or monthly basis, but tailored to very specific activities and time periods. The temporary car insurance offered by UK companies such as TempCover, DayInsure and InsureDaily is one example, with policies offered from 1 to 28 days. Of course, in addition to simply unbundling traditional service packages, new digitally based services can also be offered and micro-segmented down to highly granular levels in terms of usage, whether it's micro-payments, micro-transactions or any other form of measureable usage parameter. In addition to creating new options for digitising products and services, this is also leading to new options for monetisation, which go hand in hand with these new offerings.

2. Running or participating within industry platforms

Industry platforms are basically platform-oriented business models that consummate matches between buyers and sellers, producers and consumers, or other marketplace participants. The value being exchanged can be physical, digital or both. Some of the most well-known platform companies include Airbnb, Alibaba, Alphabet, Amazon, Apple, Facebook, LinkedIn, Microsoft, Netflix, Salesforce, Tencent, Twitter and many others. The strategic options for business model innovation in this category include setting up your own industry platform as a platform operator, participating within someone else's industry platform as a product, service or content provider, or the 'arms-dealer' model where you provide the technology building blocks and infrastructure for others to create their own platforms.

As we'll see when we take an in-depth look at industry platforms in Chapter 4, platform operators aren't just high-tech companies, there's also many non-tech industry players diving into this business model such as Philips (connected health), GE (Industrial Internet) and Bosch (manufacturing). Each of these platform operators are building out an industry platform for their specific industry, or industries in the case of GE, whereby participants can connect into the platform and utilise the various services provided.

The platform model is equally appealing to product, service and content providers since they can quickly tap into large and growing marketplaces for their services and can grow their revenues as these platforms scale up in terms of the number of participants and the number of goods and services on offer. The 'arms-dealer' model is typically most appealing to technology companies for the reasons described earlier. However, now that 'all companies are software companies', this is becoming an additional strategic option for the traditional non-tech sector as well.

3. Tapping into the sharing economy and crowdsourcing

When we look at tapping into the sharing economy, one of the main digital business models in this category is geared around offering unused or spare capacity from new or existing participants, who are willing to share their goods and services with others. This model is often built upon the platform model, in terms of how it operates and consummates matches, but it incorporates this added dimension of what's been termed the 'sharing economy' by tapping into new sources of value from new participants. Examples include Airbnb's online marketplace in the home rental industry, which enables people to list, find and rent vacation homes for a processing fee. The company has over 2 million listings in more 34,000 cities and 191 countries.[4]

Another digital business model in this category is to tap into crowdsourcing for specific organisational functions such as product innovation, product testing or customer service. The practice of open innovation, whereby companies such as Procter & Gamble (P&G) utilise crowdsourcing techniques to generate ideas for new products and services, is a good example. Through their open innovation strategy, P&G has established more than 2,000 successful agreements with innovation partners around the world.[5] Another example is Tesla, who use crowdsourcing across their over 70,000-strong customer base to assemble a database of user driving patterns and traffic patterns with over 780 million miles of data collected to date. The crowdsourcing approach also allows Tesla to test new software code covertly by observing what the software would have done if it were turned on.[6]

4. Reshaping value networks

Reshaping value networks relates to how you distribute, or re-distribute, the exchange of value among participants in your business ecosystem. This can entail new players, new roles or changes in existing roles among participants, and changes in the ways participants can connect with one another to exchange value. One of the major strategies here is often to move from a pipeline model (that is, a traditional, linear value chain) to a platform model (that is, a digital, inter-connected value chain). The industry platform and sharing economy types of models that we've just seen are good examples. Reshaping value networks can also be done in more subtle, evolutionary ways as well. For example, an organisation might be able to get closer to the customer in their industry value chain without necessarily having to move to a platform model. In digital health care, a lot of the innovation is around reshaping who pays for service and who buys service, thus changing the rules of how health care is accessed and delivered.

As we saw in Chapter 1, organisations may be able to get closer to the customer by applying big data analytics to understand their customers' preferences, needs, interests and behaviours far better than anyone else and by offering compelling applications and experiences. Collecting information about their customers' usage of products or services may enable them to monetise the data spinning around their products or services as well, by turning it into additional value-added services.

5. Creating new models for monetisation

When we look at creating new models for monetisation, the options include subscription pricing models, 'freemium' pricing models and free models, to access over ownership, and various on-demand models. The latter two of these are closely aligned with the sharing economy model, where consumers are moving more towards cost-conscious and environmentally friendly approaches where they use just what they need as opposed to buying and storing masses of products they may seldom use. According to *The Guardian*, 'Some 80% of items in UK and US homes are used less than once a month, and self-storage is now a $24B industry in the US.'[7]

As an example of access over ownership, companies such as ZipCar offer access to cars for short time periods as opposed to traditional ownership. They cater to consumers who are looking for an alternative to the costs and hassles of owning or renting a car. This is particularly beneficial for consumers who want to save money, who take public transport and only need to use a car occasionally, or who need a second car once in a while. The ZipCar example differs from traditional car rental agencies because they can offer vehicles for time periods down to 1 hour, or even 30 minutes in certain cities, and additionally charge a single fee as opposed to charging extra for petrol, insurance and daily mileage.[8] As an example of an on-demand model, companies such as TaskRabbit offer help with chores such as housework, delivery or moving.

In terms of subscription, freemium and free models, you only have to look as far as Disney, LinkedIn and Google. Disney offers an array of subscription-based services such as DisneyLife, which is a digital membership giving access to Disney movies, kids' TV box sets, books, music and apps, all in one place. LinkedIn offers free basic services and a number of plans within their premium service if you want access to enhanced features and functionality, depending on your goals. The plans support members looking to land their dream job, grow and nurture their network, unlock sales opportunities, or find and hire talent. In terms of free models, companies such as Google and Facebook offer free access to their various offerings in exchange for access to consumer data and their attention.

Creating new sources of value in new ways

If we look across all these options for business model innovation, we find that it's all about creating new sources of value in new ways. Each strategic option focuses on a slightly different aspect of this value creation and addresses a slightly different strategic question as follows:

- **Digitising products and services** – How can you deliver value through new products and services?

- **Running or participating within industry platforms** – How can you find and exchange value as a market operator or participant?

- **Tapping into the sharing economy and crowdsourcing** – How can you capture new sources of value from new players?

- **Reshaping value networks** – How can you distribute or re-distribute value among participants?

- **Creating new models for monetisation** – How can you offer or pay for value in new ways?

Table 2.1 summarises these strategic options for business model innovation and provides industry examples for each.

Table 2.1 Strategic options for digital business models with industry examples

Digital business model	Industry examples
Digitising products and services	• Converting physical products to digital equivalents (e.g. Amazon, Apple iTunes, Netflix) • Wrapping new digital services around existing physical products (e.g. GE, Nest, Pro-Form, NordicTrack) • Unbundling value propositions to make services more customised and specific (e.g. TempCover, DayInsure, InsureDaily)

(continued)

Table 2.1 (Continued)

Digital business model	Industry examples
Running or participating within industry platforms	• Operating industry platforms and aggregating value propositions (e.g. Airbnb, Alibaba, Alphabet, Amazon, Apple, Facebook, LinkedIn, Microsoft, Netflix, Salesforce, Tencent, Twitter) • Participating within industry platforms (e.g. Apple's content providers for iTunes and the App store) • 'Arms-dealer' model supplying technology for industry platforms (e.g. Cisco, Intel, Microsoft)
Tapping into the sharing economy and crowdsourcing	• Tapping into unused or spare capacity, often from new participants (e.g. Airbnb, Uber) • Crowdsourcing key functions such as product innovation, product testing and customer service (e.g. P&G, Tesla)
Reshaping value networks	• Moving from pipeline to platform business models (e.g. Airbnb, Uber) • Reshaping who pays for service and who buys service (e.g. digital health care) • Moving closer to the customer (e.g. GOV.UK's 'outside-in' approach to service delivery for UK citizens)
Creating new models for monetisation	• Subscription, freemium and free models (e.g. Disney, LinkedIn, Google, Facebook) • Access over ownership and on-demand models (e.g. ZipCar, TaskRabbit) • Micro-payments and micro-lending in financial services (e.g. Kiva)

Once an organisation has narrowed in on a specific business model innovation to pursue, one of the interesting aspects is that many traditional strategy moves can be applied to the new model. In essence, the business model itself may be totally new, but the strategy techniques to deploy and grow the model are often classic techniques that still hold true today.

We'll take a look at some of the digital business strategy moves from Apple in their Apple Pay business model, originally launched in 2014, to see how some of these classic techniques were applied to their new model.

CASE STUDY – APPLE

Classic (digital) business strategy moves from apple pay

Apple's announcement at its Worldwide Developer Conference[9] of giving shoppers even more ways to pay via its Apple Pay service was an interesting example of a set of eight classic (digital) business strategy moves the company has executed over the course of launching its service.

I've put the term 'digital' in parentheses because these are classic strategy moves that apply to both traditional business strategies as well as modern-day digital business strategies.

Here's the list of eight moves that I believe have been key to the adoption and success of the Apple Pay service in recent years:

1. Improve the (digital) customer experience: Customers typically adopt new technologies and approaches because they are faster, better or cheaper. This is the key to any disruptive change, whether it's a new product, service or entire business model. The new product or service doesn't have to have the most features and functions, but must simply be good enough and compelling enough to drive adoption and a departure from the status quo. In this case, the customer experience was improved by a radically easier way to pay; as simple as the touch of a finger. The starting point for any digital transformation is taking this outside-in perspective, looking at things from the customer's point of view, and making things simple and elegant.

2. Transform the (digital) business process: In conjunction with the first move, it's important to also re-think and re-design the business process in the new context – in this case the context of mobile payments. An improved customer experience isn't all that great if it's built on top of an old, outdated and complicated process. In this case, the ability to pay via the touch of a finger made the process about as simple as it could possibly get when compared to the traditional, physical wallet approach, while at the same time making it work with other Apple products such as the Apple Watch, prior versions of iPhones such as the 5, 5c and 5s (via the Apple Watch) and the iPad.

3. Address the (digital) barriers to adoption: As with most emerging technologies over the years, security and privacy are often at the top of the list when it comes to barriers to adoption. The Apple Pay system addressed this head on in both areas. In terms of security, the Touch ID feature enabled Apple to biometrically authenticate users as part of the payment process itself and remove the need for cashiers to see your name, credit card number or security code. Privacy was addressed via Apple deciding not to collect purchase history and not knowing what was bought, where it was bought or how much was paid for it.

4. Leverage your (digital) installed base: As opposed to attempting to introduce a new product or service to a new set of customers ('new product/new market'), it's always safer to bring a new product or service to your existing installed base, or to bring an existing product or service to new customers. That way you're dealing with one unknown instead of two, and it's more of an adjacency play. By leveraging their installed base of over 200 million iPhone 5 users (at the time), together with customers already planning to upgrade to the iPhone 6 and 6 Plus for various other reasons, Apple was able to offer the Apple Pay service without requiring customers to invest or make any changes solely for the service itself.

5. Use existing (digital) infrastructure and standards: When launching a new product or service, it's important not to require partners to make huge investments in infrastructure or to require customers to make changes that would detract from the overall value proposition of the offering. By leveraging the near field communication (NFC) standard, Apple wasn't requiring merchants to install dedicated or proprietary hardware and could ride on the contactless payments trend already underway.

6. Time your (digital) move: Another classic strategy move is to let your competitors make any first mover mistakes, let the market and/or technology mature a little further, and wait until the market timing and customer appetite is just right to launch your offering. This is a strategy that Apple has utilised time and time again whether it is music, smartphones, tablets or smart watches. Apple hasn't necessarily been the first to bring technology innovation to the table, but has innovated with design, simplicity and elegance to make its products and services highly compelling for its audience.

7. Leverage partners for (digital) credibility: In the case of a technology player making an entrance into a vertical industry ecosystem, it's important to team with industry partners to establish credibility and acceptance within the market and to complete the integrated value proposition. When Apple announced Apple Pay in September 2014,[10] it had lined up support for credit and debit cards from the three major payment networks: American Express, MasterCard and Visa, issued by some of the most popular banks, so that it could address 83 per cent of the credit card purchase volume in the US. It also had support from leading retailers so that it could address 220,000 merchant locations across the US that had contactless payments enabled.

8. Innovate (digitally) then radiate: One of the final steps in any strategy is to expand to other geographies, customers and partners. You might call this an 'innovate, then radiate' approach. Apple's announcement at its Worldwide Developer Conference in June 2015 was exactly that. The company announced support for rewards programmes and store-issued credit and debit cards with iOS 9. In addition, they announced expanding merchant acceptance to over 1 million locations in July 2015 and support for Discover in the autumn. In terms of geographic expansion, they announced expansion to the UK to work with 250,000 retail locations and the London Transit System. Continuing this geographical expansion, in December 2015 they announced a partnership with China UnionPay to bring Apple Pay to China.[11]

Key takeaways
There are a number of lessons to be learned from looking at Apple's strategic moves related to Apple Pay. One of them is that the bulk of these moves were conceived and executed pre-launch. By the time the service was announced in late 2014, it was essentially a case of methodical execution. The announcement at their Worldwide Developer Conference was simply one more step in a classic (digital) business strategy.

Finally, 'disruptive' new offerings always get a lot of debate as to the type and degree of disruption. It's interesting to note that while the Apple Pay service can be considered disruptive when compared to former payment techniques such as the use of physical wallets and credit cards, as pointed out by Juan Pablo Vazquez Sampere in the *Harvard Business Review*,[12] the business model itself is more a reseller model, since it still relies on the credit card ecosystem and does not disrupt the industry model itself. This raises the question and possibility of perhaps more strategic moves down the road – possibly targeted at this very same industry model.

RE-THINKING AND RE-DESIGNING BUSINESS PROCESSES

The goals and objectives related to re-thinking and re-designing business processes in the world of digital business are not that different from the original goals and objectives set forth by Michael M. Hammer and James A. Champy in their landmark book, *Reengineering the corporation*, written in 1993. In their book, Hammer and Champy defined business process re-engineering as:

Fundamental rethinking and radical redesign of business process to achieve dramatic improvements in critical measures of performance such as cost, service, and speed.

At the time, IT was one of the key enablers supporting business process re-design efforts. Work activities were able to be re-engineered by turning the industrial model on its head in terms of moving from simple tasks for workers connected by complex processes, to more complex tasks for workers connected by more efficient, stream-lined and automated processes. Hammer and Champy's premise was that 'to meet the contemporary demands of quality, service, flexibility, and low cost, processes must be kept simple'.

They also discerned several key characteristics and recurring themes when they studied re-engineered processes as follows:

- Several jobs are combined into one.
- Workers make decisions.
- The steps in the process are performed in a natural order.
- Processes have multiple versions.
- Work is performed where it makes the most sense.
- Checks and controls are reduced.
- Reconciliation is minimised.
- A case manager provides a single point of contact.
- Hybrid centralised–decentralised operations are prevalent.

Today's digital transformation initiatives, whether aimed at the industry level, the business model level or the process level, are all about achieving the same dramatic improvements in cost, service and speed. More than incremental process improvements, or incremental process optimisation, as we saw in Chapter 1, the digital medium allows us to completely transform and effectively 're-wire' how value gets exchanged, how work gets done and how the underlying processes get conducted.

When re-designing business processes in the digital age, we can leverage some of the same recurring themes that Hammer and Champy discerned, in addition to some new ones. For example, digital enables us to move even further along the continuum in terms of having work performed 'where it makes most sense' from the physical desk, to the desktop, to the smartphone and ultimately to the wearable. It also enables processes to 'have multiple versions', for example allowing manufacturers to move to a 'lot size of 1', whereby manufactured items can be individually crafted for specific customers to enable individualised mass production. This concept extends to the point where 'smart products', even while they are being made, know the details of their own manufacturing process and can communicate this back to the assembly line within the 'smart factory'.

If we were to come up with a similar set of recurring themes for digitally re-designed (re-engineered) business processes, we can discern several key characteristics and recurring themes as follows:

- The digital customer experience drives everything.
- Processes are highly automated and incorporate seamless hand-offs between humans and machines.
- Processes are simplified down to their most intuitive, minimal steps.
- Physical distances become irrelevant and are often completely removed from the equation.
- Processes have multiple versions and infinite configurations down to the individual customer, product or service.
- Dynamic processes are created, deployed and executed 'on the fly'.
- Real-time data informs and optimises processes.
- Fine-grained measurements enable more precise process design.
- Value propositions are aggregated across industry and company boundaries.
- Processes are massively scalable through platform business models.

This enables digital processes to be experience-centric, automated, simplified, digitised, personalised, dynamic, real time, granular, aggregated and scalable.

Table 2.2 provides some industry examples for these various characteristics. In the table, I've listed industry examples that most demonstrate each of the specific characteristics, but it's also important to note that many of the best examples combine several of these characteristics into their overall process design.

Table 2.2 Characteristics of digitally re-designed business processes with industry examples

Digital process characteristic	Industry example
Experience-centric – The digital customer experience drives everything, powered by rich combinations of technology enablers.	Streetline's 'Parker' app allows drivers to easily find parking spots via their smartphone by viewing real-time parking data, which is provided by IoT sensors and published to the cloud.
Automated – Processes are highly automated and incorporate seamless hand-offs between humans and machines.	Rethink Robotics have socialised their Baxter industrial robot by implementing anticipatory intelligence so the robot physically communicates where it's about to move, thus optimising human–machine coordination.
Simplified – Processes are simplified down to their most intuitive, minimal steps.	Apple Pay enables consumers to pay for goods and services with a single touch of their smartphone, providing both identification and payment authorisation.
Digitised – Physical distances become irrelevant and are often completely removed from the equation.	Chase's 'QuickDeposit' app enables cheque deposits from anywhere, anytime by taking photos of the front and back of the cheque via the customer's smartphone.
Personalised – Processes have multiple versions and infinite configurations down to the individual customer, product or service.	The Industry 4.0 vision for the future of manufacturing enables manufacturers to produce items down to a 'lot size of 1', with smart products specifying all details about their manufacture.
Dynamic – Dynamic processes are created, deployed and executed on the fly.	Software-defined principles enable IT leaders to dynamically manage and provision data centre services across applications, infrastructure (such as compute, network and storage) and even security.
Real time – Real-time data informs and optimises processes.	GE's Predix platform enables real-time data from locomotives and other industrial assets to be fed into their cloud-based operating system and analysed to support asset performance management and operations optimisation activities, including preventive maintenance and repair.
Granular – Fine-grained measurements enable more precise process design.	Progressive's 'Snapshot' device allows drivers to receive discounts on their monthly policy payments based on how they actually drive by recording information about the time of day, distance driven, and any hard acceleration or braking events.

(continued)

Table 2.2 (Continued)

Digital process characteristic	Industry example
Aggregated – Value propositions are aggregated across industry and company boundaries.	GOV.UK has focused on re-setting the way that services work to be unified, cross-departmental journeys (whether that's buying a vehicle, importing plants or disposing of waste).
Scalable – Processes are massively scalable through platform business models.	Uber utilised the power of the platform business model to reach a market capitalisation of over $50B in less than five years.[13]

As we'll see in Chapters 3 and 4, part of the secret to mastering digital business, and a key ingredient in some of the most successful business process re-design efforts using the 'digital medium', is utilising combinations of enabling technologies to create the most compelling digital customer experience possible. Experience-centric digital processes, by their very nature, tap into powerful combinations of emerging and disruptive technologies as their foundational building blocks. We saw this earlier in our Streetline example, which taps into data from IoT sensors, relayed to the cloud, to publish real-time parking data via a mobile app so drivers can find open parking spots.

There's a lot we can learn from studying digital business process re-design examples around a single technology enabler as well. Mobility is a great example. In the next section, we'll study some of the key scenarios around mobile process re-design that can serve as a framework for thinking about your own re-design initiatives.

Four scenarios of mobile process re-design

As organisations seek to mobile-enable internal and customer-facing applications across their enterprise, one of the most interesting topics is the whole concept of mobile process re-design. Mobile-enabling an enterprise application is about more than just mobile-enabling the old process; it's an opportunity to completely re-think and re-design the business process from the ground up in the new mobile context. In some cases, it's even an opportunity to invent entirely new business models. You could even call this the 'consumerisation of business processes', as powerful new mobile devices expand possibilities and turn traditional business processes upside down.

The objective with mobile process re-design is to think about how mobility can streamline business processes, reduce costs or even deliver entirely new services over the mobile channel. This aspect of mobility has been around for a long time, even before today's smartphones, tablets and wearables, but what's new and different is that today's devices are far more sophisticated and feature-rich – creating possibilities that simply weren't technically feasible even just a few years ago.

In exploring what might be possible within your organisation, it's worth looking at some of the scenarios already being implemented and proven in the marketplace. If we can classify these scenarios into various types of process re-design it can help illustrate some of the potential strategic levers available for chief information officers (CIOs), application portfolio managers and business leaders to apply within their mobility strategies (see Figure 2.1).

Two angles of attack in terms of mobile process re-design are clearly mobile-enabling the process (that is, making a non-mobile process mobile) and technology enabling or technology enhancing the process (that is, making an already mobile process more automated). Since mobile-enablement can be a somewhat confusing term relating to either the physical aspect of mobility (how the work is performed in terms of digital or physical process steps) or the technology aspect of mobility (how the work is performed in terms of use of mobile technologies), we'll use some new terms to describe these angles of attack:

- **Digital–physical intensity** – Relates to the level of virtualisation of the process, compared to actual physical process steps, being utilised to help digitise the process.

- **Mobile technology intensity** – Relates to the level of mobile technology, compared to other technologies, being utilised to help automate the process.

In the first case, if you increase the digital–physical intensity, you're bringing the process to the place where the work actually gets done and may be able to reduce the number of process steps. The process is optimised, since there's no need for redundant and time-consuming steps – for example, to go back to the office to enter data and so forth.

In the second case, if you increase the mobile technology intensity, you're bringing mobile technology such as tablets, smartphones and wearables to bear to help automate the process. You may already be conducting your process at the actual point of service, but bringing more technology to the table can help improve automation, cut cycle times and improve the digital customer experience.

Figure 2.1 The four scenarios of mobile process re-design

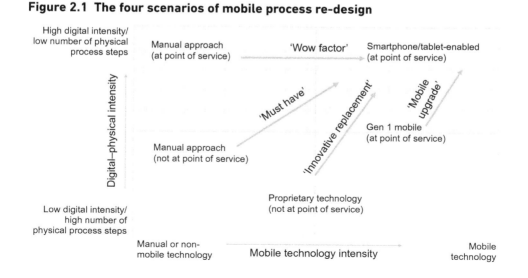

This graph presents four scenarios to consider within this simple framework of mobile technology intensity (x-axis) and digital–physical intensity (y-axis). Let's examine these in detail.

1. The 'wow factor'

This scenario relates to the use of mobile technology to replace former manual or paper-based approaches, which are already delivered at the point of service. The business benefit is typically reduced costs, faster information access, plus a 'wow factor' in cases such as customer sales and service, where interactivity and overall experience are key.

A good example in terms of reduced costs is United Airlines use of the iPad to replace their 45 lb flight bags and to provide pilots with access to charts, maps and other crucial navigation tools.[14] The business benefit in this case included the ability to save 16 million sheets of paper a year and to save 326,000 gallons of fuel in terms of weight reduction on the flights.

2. The 'must have'

This scenario relates to the biggest win possible when a manual process is totally re-designed for a new, mobile context with mobile technologies. While most of the common scenarios such as sales force automation and field force automation have already been implemented, if you find a new opportunity here the business benefits can be huge. The business benefit is typically substantial cost savings due to the new level of automation, reduced cycle times, and improved convenience and ease of use.

A classic example is the use of mobile technology in the doctor's office, where not only is the former paper-based process automated, it's also moved to the point of care so physicians and nurses can access and update patient medical records and charts while consulting side by side with their patients.

3. The 'innovative replacement'

This scenario relates to the innovative replacement of proprietary and costly technologies that are typically not mobile-enabled, with newly available features and functions built into today's next-generation devices such as tablets, smartphones and wearables.

A time-proven but classic example of innovative replacement is the cheque deposit apps from various banks such as Chase's Mobile app, which contains their QuickDeposit service.[15] This service lets customers take a photo of the front and back of their cheques and then verify the deposit details on their device to make a rapid deposit from the comfort of their homes, replacing the need to drive to the bank and use the ATM for the same purpose. Square's solution for merchants to take mobile payments is another example – in this case replacing cash registers – and one that garnered them recognition as one of the most innovative companies on the lists of both *Fast Company* and *MIT Technology Review*. Other examples in this category include the use of built-in features such as Global Positioning System (GPS) and compasses, or even biometrics capabilities to replace former standalone equivalents.

4. The 'mobile upgrade'

This scenario is similar to the 'innovative replacement', but upgrades an existing mobile technology as opposed to a proprietary, non-mobile technology of some kind such as an

ATM or cash register. Business benefits typically include cost savings and substantially improved usability.

An example here is the Dallas Museum of Art's (DMA's) use of smartphones to provide interactive museum tours to visitors as a supplement to their use of handheld audio tour devices. The DMA was one of the first to offer this capability back in 2010 and is continually expanding this service to additional collections and exhibitions within the museum. Another example is the growing use of consumer-oriented tablets for field service purposes such as delivery routing, as opposed to former proprietary mobile technologies.

Key takeaways

One of the benefits of these scenarios is that they may help to illuminate some of the strategic questions to be thinking about related to mobile process re-design and how to consumerise your business processes. Questions such as, 'What mobile technologies can we upgrade?', 'What proprietary technologies can we totally replace?' or 'How can we re-think the end-user experience?' Of course, the key question is, 'What business processes or even business models can we totally reinvent and re-design to do business in a whole new manner?' Is the consumerisation of business processes the next step after the consumerisation of IT? Only time will tell, but the emerging scenarios in recent years are starting to paint a compelling picture.

KEY TAKEAWAYS FOR CHAPTER 2

- The number of strategic options for business model innovation in the age of digital are many and varied. They range from digitising products and services, to running or participating within industry 'platforms', to tapping into the sharing economy and crowdsourcing, to reshaping value networks, to creating new models for monetisation. If we look across all these options for business model innovation, we find that it's all about creating new sources of value in new ways.

- Once an organisation has narrowed in on a specific business model innovation to pursue, one of the interesting aspects is that many traditional strategy moves can be applied to the new model. In essence the business model itself may be totally new, but the strategy techniques to deploy and grow the model are often classic techniques that still hold true today.

- In terms of re-thinking and re-designing business processes, there are a number of recurring themes and key characteristics that enable digital processes to trump traditional processes by being experience-centric, automated, simplified, digitised, personalised, dynamic, real time, granular, aggregated and scalable. Many of the best examples combine several of these characteristics into their overall process design.

- To help you think further about re-design efforts within your own organisation, there are four strategic pathways for re-designing mobile business processes. These pathways are focused on improving digital–physical intensity as well as mobile technology intensity and include what we can describe as the 'wow factor', the 'must have', the 'innovative replacement' and the 'technology upgrade'.

3 MAXIMISING THE POTENTIAL OF TODAY'S DISRUPTIVE TECHNOLOGIES FOR DIGITAL BUSINESS

Any sufficiently advanced technology is indistinguishable from magic.

Arthur C. Clarke[1]

One of the keys to maximising the potential of today's disruptive technologies lies in exploiting them in powerful combinations. This chapter introduces the set of emerging and disruptive technologies – including SMAC technologies, plus wearables, robotics and the IoT – that are serving as foundational building blocks for new, digitally enabled business models. We look beyond some of the commonly cited examples of tech giants and business scenarios for each disruptive technology, to explore how leading organisations such as Uber, GOV.UK and the Mercedes AMG Petronas Formula One team are using precise combinations of these technologies to unlock powerful new forms of business value.

SMAC AND THE EVOLUTION OF IT

To provide some background context in terms of how we've arrived at today's diverse set of disruptive technologies for digital business, it's worth looking back to see how the IT industry has evolved over time. Every 15 years or so, the IT industry has witnessed new innovations in computing that have changed the way IT services are delivered to business and end users. After the mainframe era, mini-computing era, personal computer and client-server era, and the internet era (or more correctly, the 'web' era), we're now in what many call the fifth wave of corporate IT. This fifth wave is characterised by a new master IT architecture comprised of SMAC technologies at its core foundation.

> A combination of forces – such as mobility, cloud, big data and social technology – means fleet-of-foot start-ups have been able to move into territory that is traditionally owned by larger enterprises.[2]
>
> (Dr Mark Samuels, n.d.)

One of the key changes over time, throughout all these evolutions, has been the exponentially increasing processing power of computers, and the steady growth in the number of computing devices, applications and users. Table 3.1 shows the rough magnitude of these changes across the various computing eras – dates and numbers are approximate just to give a sense of the order of magnitude.

Table 3.1 IT industry evolution in terms of computers, applications and users

IT era	Dates (approximate)	Computers (approximate)	Applications (approximate)	Users (approximate)
Mainframe	1950–65	~100,000	Thousands	Millions
Mini-computing	1965–80	~10M	Thousands	Tens of millions
PC and client-server	1980–95	~100M	Tens of thousands	Hundreds of millions
Web	1995–2010	~1B	Hundreds of thousands	Billion
SMAC	2010–25?	Tens of billions	Millions	Billions

Source: Various sources including Cognizant, IDC, Unisys.

It should be noted that each era often builds and extends upon the previous era. The era simply marks the approximate period that the specific technologies were the predominant technologies. For example, we still have mainframes and client-server applications in the typical large enterprise, and today SMAC technologies are building upon web technologies.

The real promise of today's digital business technologies – built on top of the SMAC foundation – is not necessarily their individual contributions or their cost savings and process efficiencies for IT, but their potential to support the continued digitisation, automation and transformation of business models and processes. According to many, we're moving into a new 'digital industrial revolution'.

With the SMAC stack well established as the foundational set of technologies for next-generation IT architectures, many are now asking what the next evolution of this platform will look like and how it will evolve to support and enable digital business in the years ahead.

BEYOND SMAC: THE NEW PLATFORM FOR DIGITAL BUSINESS

As we discussed in Chapter 1 in the section on preparing for the digital disruption that's coming to your industry, understanding the make-up of this new platform is vital for companies wishing to either create digital disruption in their industry or pro-actively respond to it.

When SMAC technologies first hit the scene several years ago, they were broadly applicable and highly disruptive to enterprise IT. The next wave of disruptive technologies, some mature and some emerging, are now broadly applicable and highly disruptive to business models and processes.

So, from being a former 'disruption' to enterprise IT, SMAC technologies are now becoming the essential building blocks of a new platform for digital business initiatives. This new platform for digital business is comprised of the familiar SMAC technologies, but adds in personas and context, intelligent automation, the IoT and, of course, cyber security. In addition, mobility is evolving and embracing wearable technologies, and the cloud is evolving and embracing broader concepts such as hybrid IT and software-defined data centres.

Table 3.2 lists these foundational building blocks for the new platform for digital business and provides an accompanying high-level description of the business value that each technology brings to the table.

Table 3.2 Foundational building blocks for the new platform for digital business

Foundational building blocks	Business value
Social computing	• Social computing enables connection to a new generation and is a new effectiveness frontier for workforce productivity. • Social computing can transform work processes in functions such as product development, operations and distribution, sales and marketing, and customer service, as well as across the entire enterprise.
Mobility and wearables	• Mobility is allowing us to re-imagine the way we access and consume information, communicate, and conduct business transactions – including payments. • Wearables (including smart glasses and watches) and augmented reality (AR) applications provide the next breakthrough in customer experience, instant information and hands-free process optimisation.
Analytics	• Insights from big data and real-time analytics can help make better decisions, improve efficiencies and gain competitive advantage.
Cloud and hybrid IT	• Cloud technologies and platforms are providing agility and flexibility, and cost savings via software-, infrastructure-, and platform-as-a-service delivery models. • End users and consumers typically gain the benefits of improved productivity, reduced costs, easy access and a pay-as-you-go subscription model.

(continued)

Table 3.2 (Continued)

Foundational building blocks	Business value
Personas and context	• Personas and context help organisations deliver a compelling, new digital customer experience. • They help organisations better understand the customer's context including preferences, needs, interests, behaviours, location, language and sentiment so they can deliver a highly curated experience.
Intelligent automation	• Cognitive systems and intelligent automation are helping organisations reduce costs and dependence on labour-based processes and optimise their service efficiencies. • Advances in machine learning, expert systems and robotics are leading to automation opportunities in both physical and virtual (software) scenarios.
IoT	• The IoT enables new business models and transformed processes based on real-time data and analytics. • Intelligent information can be shared across machines, networks, individuals or groups to facilitate intelligent collaboration and better decision making.
Cyber security	• New cyber security solutions are helping to secure the next wave of IT 'assets' including social, mobile, cloud and the IoT. • These IT assets, external to the traditional security 'perimeter', all multiply the number of internet vulnerabilities, necessitating new approaches to securing the digital enterprise.

Collectively, these technologies can be utilised to assemble a platform ecosystem of on-demand services providing a palette of options for digital business outcomes (see Figure 3.1). Based on your perspective, you'll select powerful combinations of these technologies to achieve target business outcomes such as improving the digital customer experience, enhancing the digital workplace, transforming business processes, optimising infrastructure, simplifying management and implementing an adaptive cyber security defence posture.

If you're a chief marketing officer (CMO) or business leader, you'll likely focus on initiatives such as applying digital transformation to launch new business models, products and services; enhancing the digital customer experience to improve customer loyalty and revenues; transforming business processes to reduce costs, improve productivity and differentiate offerings; or obtaining insights from analytics to make better

Figure 3.1 The new platform for digital business

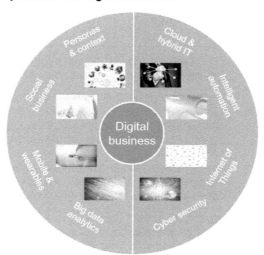

decisions, improve efficiencies and gain competitive advantage. In this case, you'll select mostly from technologies to the left of the circle, but tap into those on the right as needed as well.

If you're a CIO, you'll likely focus on the aforementioned business initiatives in partnership with your business colleagues, plus core IT initiatives such as establishing a mission-critical infrastructure with increased agility, flexibility, manageability and security. In this latter case, you'll select mostly from technologies to the right of the circle.

Overall, this new platform can be used as a frame of reference for digital business transformation in terms of the key IT capabilities – both technologies and approaches – needed to support your target business outcomes. Here are six key characteristics of the platform and how the model can help with your planning:

- **Foundational building blocks** – Key disruptive technologies serve as foundational building blocks – some mature, some emerging. The SMAC stack will likely represent the core building blocks, but you'll add other technologies based on your specific innovation needs and objectives. The IoT and intelligent automation (including both software and physical robots) will likely play a big role, but so will other enablers such as 3D printing and machine learning.

- **Common groupings of services** – Common groupings of services such as those provided by SDDCs can address specific business objectives and accelerate time-to-market. Rather than build out every foundational element in support of a particular business objective, you may be able to find off-the-shelf capabilities where the various disruptive technologies have been pre-integrated and pre-packaged so you can put them to work immediately. For example, you may find a SDDC capability that has already pre-integrated the traditional SDDC components of 'compute', 'network' and 'storage', with additional elements such as software-defined security and software-defined management.

- **Ecosystem of services** – Rather than a monolithic platform that integrates everything, the future platform will consist of a highly virtualised, highly distributed, ecosystem of services from best-in-class providers – some of these capabilities you'll build yourself, others you'll outsource or subscribe to as-a-service, and others you may co-create with partners.

- **Framework for assessment** – The platform provides a simple framework for assessing digital business proficiency and opportunity areas. For example, are you adequately leveraging each of these disruptive technology enablers in support of your business objectives? Perhaps you're totally up to speed in leveraging the SMAC stack, but what about the IoT and areas such as wearables or robotic process automation?

- **Digital services lifecycle** – Mastery of the digital services lifecycle is going to become a key competency for organisations to grow their business and build sustainable competitive advantage in the years ahead. It's no longer sufficient to have an innovative set of products or services, you have to be a master of how you design, develop, deploy, manage and continually evolve your digital services as well. This is where capabilities such as agile and DevOps come into play so that you can quickly develop and deploy your new digital services. Agile is a collection of evolving delivery and management frameworks for dynamic and innovative delivery environments – like IT deliveries.[3] DevOps focuses on improving collaboration between development and operations teams through the adoption of agile, lean practices in the context of a system-oriented approach.[4]

- **The agile journey to the new platform** – Since IT will be a hybrid environment for quite some time, it will be important to interoperate across the two divides of the current state environment and this future vision. An agile, iterative journey to the future platform should be driven by specific business outcomes enabled by the appropriate sub-set of disruptive technologies. For example, an organisation might undergo several tracks, or work streams, in parallel – with an iterative approach to reduce risk and deliver early benefits. One track might be around optimising existing infrastructure and simplifying management and a parallel track might be around improving the digital customer experience and transforming business processes.

All in all, the new platform for digital business can be useful in thinking about the additional technology enablers, beyond the SMAC stack, that can add value and competitive advantage for digital business initiatives. In addition, one of the key points is that these technology enablers can be used in powerful combinations to support your target business objectives. For example, in digital workplace initiatives you may decide to 'instrument the human' with wearables and sensors and also 'socialise the machine' with natural language interfaces and the ability to collaboratively access and provision robotic functions via social networks. This will help to optimise the blend of human–machine participation and interaction within your re-designed business processes for the digital workplace.

If we apply the model to some of today's most interesting start-ups and next-generation business models, you'll find they apply many, if not all, of these technology enablers as part of their innovative approach. The following three case studies provide examples of how Uber, the UK Government and the Mercedes AMG Petronas Formula One team approach digital transformation by using precise combinations of enabling technology, a platform approach as part of their operating model, and a mastery of digital service design and delivery.

CASE STUDY – UBER

Decoding UBER's platform for digital business

If we look at the foundational technologies behind Uber's business model, we find the same set of emerging and disruptive technologies in our model. Uber's model is about more than just a mobile app on a smartphone and actually combines SMAC as well as the latest techniques around agile service development and DevOps (see Figure 3.2). All of this is delivered via a 'platform' business model that consummates matches – in this case between passengers and drivers – in a similar fashion to other well-known platform companies such as Airbnb, Alibaba, Alphabet, Amazon, Apple, Facebook, LinkedIn, Microsoft, Netflix, Salesforce, Tencent, Twitter and many others.

At the core of the business model, of course, is the mobile app that lets consumers request a ride with the push of a button and track the driver's progress to their location. Social features come into play in terms of rider ratings and driver feedback to help ensure 'high quality, highly rated transportation providers and drivers'.[5] Social features are also used so that passengers can share their ETA with friends and family. Uber's analytic model sets prices for rides based on distance, car type and demand period. Cloud computing comes into play in terms of Uber's as-a-service infrastructure, which operates in over 450 cities worldwide.

In addition to the core foundational technologies that Uber utilises, as per our model, two other key elements to the overall approach include their platform approach (see Chapter 4) as well as their approach to mastering the digital services lifecycle (see Chapter 12). The platform approach in terms of consummating matches between passengers and drivers enables Uber to scale their business rapidly, since they are tapping into the so-called 'sharing economy' of unused capacity and are simply providing the transaction platform to enable these matches to occur. The digital services lifecycle concept, something I term 'digital services mastery', relates to the ability of organisations to master how they design, develop, deploy, manage and continually evolve their digital services.

Even with the best set of enabling technologies and the best platform business model in the world, organisations still need to be able to respond rapidly to changing customer needs and market dynamics, and they need to be able to deploy and iterate their digital services quickly and efficiently at speed and at scale. By employing techniques such as agile and DevOps, Uber is able to iterate rapidly in terms of experimenting with new features, or even entire new service offerings, and is able to quickly place applications into production once they're developed.

Figure 3.2 Uber's enabling technologies mapped to the new platform for digital business

'DevOps enables the whole engineering org to iterate at top speed in an open, decentralised environment'

As-a-service infrastructure operates in over 200 cities and 50 countries worldwide

'Systems management and automation is the name of the game here in development, testing, staging and production'

Digitised value chain includes ability to track the car that is coming to pick you up on your phone screen and ability to pay using your credit card

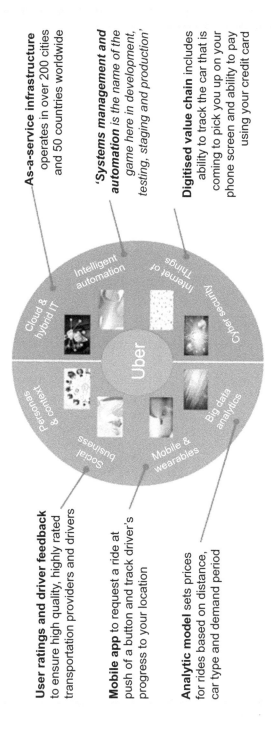

User ratings and driver feedback to ensure high quality, highly rated transportation providers and drivers

Mobile app to request a ride at push of a button and track driver's progress to your location

Analytic model sets prices for rides based on distance, car type and demand period

'Corner store' delivery example of **agile service development** – *'Limited time only experience – but the more you love it, the more likely it will last'*

CASE STUDY – UK GOVERNMENT

Decoding GOV.UK's platform for digital business

The Government Digital Service (GDS) is part of the UK Cabinet Office and is leading the digital transformation of government. The GDS is a centre of excellence in digital, technology and data, collaborating with UK government departments to help them with their own transformation. The GDS works with them to build platforms, standards and digital services. In addition to running GOV.UK, the authoritive place to find government services and information, the GDS builds platforms such as GOV.UK Verify, works to ensure that government data is good data and helps departments provide their staff with better value technology that's more of a tool and less of a barrier.[6] The GDS has won numerous design awards and is a recognised world leader in public sector digital innovation, serving as a model for many countries worldwide including the US, Australia and New Zealand.

Against a 2009–10 baseline, in 2014–15 the Cabinet Office helped government save £1.7 billion through digital and technology transformation as a direct result of work done across government by departmental teams building digital services and making better use of technology.[7] As an example, some of the significant advances in implementing digital transformation over the last UK parliament have included:

- Over 98% of driving tests are now booked online.
- Eighty-five per cent of self-assessment filing is done through online channels.
- Twelve million people have registered to vote using a new digital service.

The GDS' approach to digital transformation incorporates an 'outside in' approach to provide an authentic voice of government on the web with new behaviours, skills and capabilities, powered by innovative technology to get to the future state. As per our model for mastering digital business, two other key elements of their approach, in addition to combinations of innovative technology, include their platform approach (see Chapter 4) as well as their approach to mastering the digital services lifecycle (see Chapter 12). To achieve this, the GDS incorporates a focus on shared resources via a 'government as a platform' approach to provide a common infrastructure and set of componentry to rapidly assemble new digital services, coupled with a focus on people and capability to enable more iterative and incremental delivery models.

Outside-in approach

According to Stephen Foreshew-Cain, Executive Director of the GDS, what was particularly disruptive about GOV.UK was not the use of innovative technology so much as the consistent, authentic voice of government that the site has enabled.[8] To understand the magnitude of the change in terms of how the UK Government has transformed itself via technology, it's helpful to look at how government utilised technology in the past.

When the civil service was created in the mid-19th century, and up until fairly recently, technology was seen as something government buys. It wasn't seen as a core competency. As technology became mainstream, government didn't respond and found itself in a position where technology was a first order problem when it should have been a fourth order problem. Government agencies had a presence on the web, but disparate technologies were dictating the experience, and agency websites had very different voices, fractured interactions and limited branding.

Working with government departments and agencies, the GDS changed this by bringing the web properties of 24 ministerial departments and 331 other agencies and public bodies together in GOV.UK. The idea was to enable citizens to have a consistent, authentic experience regardless of which service they were using and to move to a more modern digital service estate while recognising that many services were 10 or more years old.

To undertake the transformation, the GDS took an adaptive and iterative approach by starting with alpha and beta versions of GOV.UK, to prove the concept and make a compelling case for ministers, before moving GOV.UK into production. In terms of their 'outside-in' approach, the GDS has focused on re-setting the way that services work to be unified, cross-department journeys (whether that's buying a vehicle, importing plants or disposing of waste), as well as creating 'service patterns' that provide consistent standards for the way a repeated activity should work for both users and government.[9] Today, GOV.UK operates approximately 806 services, with over 2.38 billion completed transactions per year.[10]

Government as a platform

The goal of government as a platform has been not just cost savings and efficiency improvements, but to reduce the cycle time between policy design and service implementation. By providing a common infrastructure, with reusable services such as notification and licensing, and componentry to assemble these services, the GDS has been able to assemble and deploy new digital services for UK citizens in much shorter time frames. Some of the current platform services include GOV.UK Verify for identity assurance, GOV.UK Pay for processing payments, and GOV.UK Notify for helping government service teams send text messages, emails or letters to users.

Government as a platform also encompasses 'registers' work whereby the law instructs government to establish, maintain or keep a register, which is an authoritative list of information. By simplifying and standardising how data is stored and accessed, the registrars who are responsible for the data can focus more on their domain-specific tasks.[11]

A good example of an improved digital service has been the process of booking a prison visit. There was a policy to make these visits more accessible and easier to set up. Evidence suggested that when prisoners had regular visits with family members, there were better outcomes for both the prisoners and the overall system. By assembling a new prison visit booking service that was easier to use, more accessible via digital channels, and made up of component services such as identity and scheduling, the booking service saw an uptick of visits of about 10%.

Digital services mastery

In addition to his responsibility for building digital infrastructure for government, Mr Foreshew-Cain is also Head of Function, which means he is responsible for defining the skills, capabilities and standards needed for service development and deployment. The team works on the principle that approaches such as agile and DevOps must be adopted to be able to quickly and rapidly iterate services in line with policy. The team is working to make this approach the new normal and to chunk down work activities so they can be quickly tested and validated. As an example, any technology spend over certain thresholds must come to the GDS for review. The team starts with a discovery phase to better understand user needs, and then progresses through alpha and beta phases. This helps to prove that the policy intent can be successfully delivered via solution development.

Moving forwards

With this set of capabilities in place, the GDS team is now focusing on going wholesale in terms of scaling across government. The goal is to 'help departments work together to transform government to meet user needs'.[12] Three themes underpinning this effort are standards and assurance, shared resources, and people and capability. In the longer term, the GDS believes that digital transformation has the 'potential to radically alter the structure of government – not just the services it provides, not just the way it builds and maintains them, but the way it operates itself'.[13]

CASE STUDY – MERCEDES AMG PETRONAS

Digital business lessons from the world of Formula One

Figure 3.3 Printed with the kind permission of Mercedes AMG Petronas Formula One

In addition to the blistering excitement of race day, the world of Formula One is well known for its technology innovation and advancements that later find their way into the consumer car industry. Examples include a multitude of innovations related to engines, transmission, braking and safety.

With all the interest in digital transformation in the business world, what can the world of Formula One, where results are measured in thousandths of a second, teach us about emerging technologies and how to manage, combine and optimise them to deliver competitive advantage?

According to Matt Harris, Head of IT at the Mercedes AMG Petronas Formula One team, there are a number of business objectives his team has to address. First, the goal of IT is to support and improve the business as a whole. The Formula One team doesn't sell anything, since the 'product', in this case, goes around the track. IT therefore focuses on providing and operating the core, car-enabling technologies for race performance as well as for the team's website and worldwide fan base.

The use of SMAC therefore comes into play in a diverse set of scenarios:

- In terms of the fan base, the team supports over 10.5 million Facebook fans and over 1.2 million Twitter followers.
- Mobility, analytics and cloud all play a role across both the racing and fan base aspects of the operation as the organisation generates about 6 terabytes (TB) a day as a business and an additional ½ TB on race weekends.

It's all about the analytics
One of the key enabling technologies from a racing perspective is data analytics. According to Harris, the team collects more data now within a single race weekend than they did across every race weekend from 1998 to 2006 combined. Given approximately 16 to 19 races per Formula One racing season, this equates to over 150 times the data volume being collected compared to prior years.

Whether its tyre temperature, degradation or many other factors, the team is always looking for the next way to measure and improve. This often means collecting higher resolution data while striving to make sensors lighter and more accurate. With an average of 200 sensors used on each of their F1 W06 Hybrid cars during the Grand Prix event, sensor weight is measured in fractions of grams. During practice sessions on Fridays, there can be even more sensors on the car as the team collects data about aerodynamics and other factors that can aid learning and optimisation of race-day performance.

Much like the corporate world, collecting and analysing data in Formula One is always a compromise in terms of how much you can consume, what to evaluate and how quickly you can act on your insights. The FIA, the sport's regulatory body, imposes rules concerning use of telemetry data and also how many team members can actually go to the track, while use of sensors is limited in many areas so teams can't use trick software coding to cheat the rules. In addition, teams are now restricted to up to 60 staff at the track – down from over 100 in prior years – so that means a limited number of eyes to look at the data.

Interestingly, when it comes to monitoring the drivers' vital signs, the team uses a more analogue approach, with verbal communications between driver and pit lane as opposed to a large number of automated sensors. So it's a case of applying technology where it can lend the most impact as opposed to trying to measure and digitise everything possible.

One of the most recent innovations related to the team's use of telemetry has been the ability to download race car telemetry data via Wi-Fi using 5 GHz spectrum through their partnership with Qualcomm. This enables the team to 'make better use of limited practice sessions and spend more time testing the configuration of the vehicle'. The move to higher frequency 5 GHz spectrum enables much faster data transfer including data from thermal imaging tyre cameras.

Seeking the next technology enablers

So what are the additional technology enablers that the team uses beyond SMAC? How is the team applying enablers such as the IoT, 3D printing and machine learning?

The IoT clearly comes into play around the team's use of sensors. The emphasis, as described earlier, is not only around data collection to improve speed, efficiency and vehicle safety, but around optimising the physical characteristics of the sensors and their positioning in the race car environment. This is a valuable lesson for the corporate world in terms of thinking strategically about what IoT sensors you need, where to position them and how the data can drive real-time outcomes.

According to Harris, the team has been at the leading edge of 3D printing for around 15 years now, if not more. This is in stark contrast to today's corporate organisations who, for the most part, are just starting to explore and deploy the technology. On the race cars themselves, the team has been using 3D printing for about five to six years for some of the less critical components such as non-load-bearing items.

Machine learning and predictive analytics is an area in which Harris wants to continue to improve in the years ahead. The team is interested in what new computer-generated insights can be provided to human analysts in order to constantly explore new perspectives and ideas.

When it comes to other automotive innovations, Harris expects to see efficiency technologies such as energy recovery systems migrate through to road cars much as innovations in car safety migrated through to road cars in prior years. Of course, some of the current innovations in road cars, such as self-driving capabilities and certain safety systems, purposefully won't migrate in the other direction because Formula One also places a premium on the human element in terms of driver skill and ability.

Achieving world-leading performance

In 2016, the Mercedes AMG Petronas Formula One Team wrapped up the first and second place slots in the Drivers' Championship, with Nico Rosberg and Lewis Hamilton respectively, and the overall Constructors' Championship.

An interesting takeaway from their IT strategy is perhaps that to achieve world-leading performance for the business, you don't necessarily have to be a world leader on the bleeding edge of every single technology enabler. It's more a case of being – or striving to become – a world leader and innovator in the areas that matter, and being a fast follower in the rest.

This should be encouraging news for corporate IT departments looking to get a digital business edge from today's latest tech trends. Pick the mix of technology enablers you need to succeed, place your bets and deploy your resources appropriately.

Overall, when we study leading organisations such as Uber, GOV.UK and the Mercedes AMG Petronas Formula One team we find they all share a common DNA in terms of their approach to digital transformation. Whether it's operating taxi services in over 450 cities worldwide, helping the UK Government save £1.7 billion for taxpayers, or winning the Formula One Driver's and Constructor's Championships, they all have three key elements in common. They all apply precise combinations of enabling technology to unlock new sources of business value, utilise a platform approach as part of their business or operating model, and have become masters of digital service design and deployment.

KEY TAKEAWAYS FOR CHAPTER 3

- One of the keys to maximising the potential of today's disruptive technologies lies in exploiting them in powerful combinations. A new set of emerging and disruptive technologies are serving as foundational building blocks for new, digitally enabled business models.

- This new platform for digital business is comprised of the familiar SMAC technologies, but adds in personas and context, intelligent automation, the IoT and, of course, cyber security. In addition, mobility is evolving and embracing wearable technologies, and the cloud is evolving and embracing broader concepts such as hybrid IT and SDDCs.

- Collectively, these technologies can be utilised to assemble a platform ecosystem of on-demand services providing a palette of options for digital business outcomes.

- Based on your perspective, you'll select powerful combinations of these technologies to achieve target business outcomes such as improving the digital customer experience, enhancing the digital workplace, transforming business processes, optimising infrastructure, simplifying management and implementing an adaptive cyber security defence posture.

- Even with the best set of enabling technologies and the best platform business model in the world, organisations still need to be able to respond rapidly to changing customer needs and market dynamics, and they need to be able to deploy and iterate their digital services quickly and efficiently at speed and at scale.

4   THE NEW PLATFORM ECOSYSTEM FOR DIGITAL BUSINESS

> Platform companies are emerging as important engines of innovation. They are increasingly at the cutting edge of rapid worldwide digital transformation.
>
> Peter C. Evans, The Center for Global Enterprise[1]

In the previous chapter we explored how various emerging and disruptive technologies are coming together to serve as the foundational building blocks for disruptions in the form of new, digitally enabled business models, processes, products and services. We saw how organisations such as Uber, GOV.UK and the Mercedes AMG Petronas Formula One Team are leveraging these technologies to deliver digitally transformed business models and processes that enable world-leading performance and results.

In this chapter, we'll dive deeper into the power of exploiting these technology combinations for specific business objectives across the organisation as well as the power of exploiting digital business ecosystem and platform approaches that are fast becoming the 'dominant' go-to-market business model. According to Peter C. Evans, Vice President at The Center for Global Enterprise, and one of the original authors of GE's visionary *Industrial internet*[2] paper back in 2012, 'Platform companies are emerging as important engines of innovation. They are increasingly at the cutting edge of rapid worldwide digital transformation.'

It is this mix of disruptive technologies, platform business models, together with a mastery of digital services – in terms of how digital services are designed, developed, deployed, managed and continually evolved – that really sets today's digital business leaders head and shoulders above the rest of the field. These elements are therefore at the heart of truly mastering digital business and crafting a successful strategy and roadmap for the years ahead.

EXPLOITING THE POWER OF TECHNOLOGY COMBINATIONS

As we think about various digital business objectives ranging from improving the digital customer experience, to transforming the digital workplace, to optimising digital infrastructure and simplifying management, we can see that different technology combinations come into play. Organisations can select the appropriate sub-set of building blocks, in the form of these distinct technology enablers, based on their target business outcomes.

Today's applications are driven by more than SMAC, and often incorporate and integrate many additional features and capabilities. These are what research firm IDC calls 'technology accelerators'[3] and they have the potential to radically extend digital capabilities and applications. Our reference model in this book for the new platform for digital business, as shown in the previous chapter, includes SMAC technologies as well as personas and context, intelligent automation, the IoT and, of course, cyber security. In addition, as we saw earlier, mobility is evolving and embracing wearable technologies and AR applications, and the cloud is evolving and embracing broader concepts such as hybrid IT and SDDCs. While these eight technologies comprise the core of the new platform for digital business, other technology enablers such as 3D printing come into play as well in specific scenarios and industries.

We'll now explore some of these target business outcomes, and the requisite technology enablers, to provide some examples of what's included and how they can be combined to deliver transformative business value.

Improving the digital customer experience

When we think about improving the digital customer experience we typically think about SMAC enablers, as well as personas and context, and robust cyber security as follows:

- **Social** – To enable customers to share, be heard and be informed via social channels.

- **Mobile** – To enable customer access anytime, anywhere with re-designed business processes for faster, improved experience.

- **Analytics** – To enable customers to interactively analyse their data and be provided with recommendations to help them make informed decisions.

- **Cloud** – To enable customers to access services on demand in a flexible, pay-as-you-go model.

- **Personas and context** – To understand the customers' context including preferences, needs, interests, behaviours, location, language and sentiment via a highly personalised and contextualised experience.

- **Cyber security** – To enable customer safety with privacy and security integrated into the full end-to-end process by design.

As an example, the Snapshot application from Progressive Insurance,[4] a US-based insurance company, allows drivers to receive discounts on their monthly policy payments based on how they actually drive as opposed to traditional factors such as where they live and the kind of car they drive. The Snapshot device fits into the car's on-board diagnostics (OBD)-II port. For each trip the driver makes, Snapshot records information about the time of day, distance driven, and any hard acceleration or braking events and sends it to Progressive's central repository.

To calculate potential savings, Progressive looks at items such as how often the driver accelerates or brakes rapidly (defined as accelerations or decelerations faster than 7mph/second), how many miles they drive each day, and also how often they drive between midnight and 4 a.m., which is a particularly risky time for accidents. Drivers can then log in to an online application to see their results and receive feedback on how to become an even safer driver.

From a 'tech combinations' perspective, the application combines technology elements of a mobile device, extensive data analytics, a cloud-based application, and 'badges' for good driving which can be shared via the driver's social networks. Progressive takes the social element even further by awarding a 'Best Driver Ever' title to the driver with the biggest potential Snapshot savings percentage. The driver's 'context' clearly comes into play in this example, since the entire application is focused on actual driving behaviour as monitored in real time by the Snapshot device.

As we'll see in Chapter 8, 'Enhancing the digital customer experience', next-generation applications may well include one or more additional enablers as follows:

- **IoT** – To enable users and applications to access and physically control IoT devices in both consumer and industrial scenarios.

- **Wearables** – To enable users and applications to take advantage of wearable devices such as smart glasses and smart watches in terms of hands-free process optimisation and convenience.

- **Intelligent automation** – To deliver smart services by applying intelligent analytics and algorithms, including artificial intelligence (AI), to understand and anticipate the customers' likely needs based upon their context and historical behaviour.

As an example, the Ring™ Video Doorbell[5] is essentially an IoT device that lets home-owners answer the door from anywhere using a wireless video doorbell. The device includes motion sensors, a high definition (HD) camera, a microphone and speakers, in addition to the actual physical doorbell, letting homeowners receive mobile alerts when movement is detected or when the doorbell is pressed. Homeowners can then see and speak with visitors from anywhere via an app on their smartphone. In addition, Ring's partnerships with a number of electronic lock companies enable homeowners to unlock their front doors to allow visitors to enter while they are away.

In terms of 'tech combinations', Ring uses an IoT device, a mobile app, video recording in the cloud, as well as allowing users to share access with additional users by simply entering their email address. When multiple users are connected to the Ring Doorbell, all users are notified of activity via push notifications. As per our earlier Snapshot example, we see the familiar combination of SMAC technologies, but with the addition of multiple IoT devices in this smart home scenario.

We'll explore strategies for enhancing the digital customer experience in more detail in Chapter 8. The key point here, however, is that various technology enablers can come together to deliver a completely new customer experience and set of capabilities (i.e. new services) that taps into the power, simplicity and convenience that each one of these enablers has to offer. Traditional business processes, such as car insurance and home security in these specific examples, have been re-thought and re-designed in the context of the new art of the possible these technologies enable.

While SMAC capabilities are now expected by default in leading consumer applications, the new competitive battleground will be fought with new weaponry that taps into the power of personas and context, wearables and AR, the IoT and intelligent automation.

Transforming the digital workplace

When we think about transforming the digital workplace, we see a similar set of technology enablers as we saw for improving the digital customer experience. The building blocks for next-generation applications typically include SMAC technologies together with one or more enablers such as IoT, wearables and AR, and intelligent automation.

In the IoT arena, radio frequency identification (RFID) tags have long been used for high-value asset tracking particularly in supply chain scenarios in the military as well as commercial operations. You may well remember the famous 'RFID mandates' from vendors such as Walmart as well as the US Department of Defense back in the early 2000s. As one of the early IoT 'devices' on the market all those years ago, RFID tags provided the identity, description and location of an object – at the item, case and pallet level – as well as having the ability to capture and share other readings such as temperature, pressure and shock throughout the object's journey along the supply chain.

Much of this supply chain focus around RFID at the time was directed towards supply chain optimisation in terms of minimising the so-called 'bull-whip effect', where retailers and distributors carry too much inventory in excess of demand. In other scenarios, RFID tags can help to support anti-counterfeiting efforts by providing a unique ID for the item, such as certain classes of pharmaceuticals, and additional sensors can help to ensure that items such as perishable goods are kept within their environmental tolerances while in transit.

Today, new IoT applications are emerging in the workplace to digitally optimise work processes and provide instant information and total recall for next-generation workers and employers. Many of these applications are designed to track and monitor worker behaviour for a variety of health and wellbeing, safety and efficiency goals.

As an example, the connected police officer of the future may use a variety of IoT devices and sensors to detect environmental hazards, provide biometric health monitoring, monitor his or her gun holster to detect when the weapon is drawn, and capture and stream live video. Back in 2015, the UK's Metropolitan Police Service (MPS) started the largest urban trial of body worn video (BWV) use in the world, incorporating the use of 500 cameras by response officers and 500 cameras being used within specialist roles such as Firearms, Tactical Support Group, Dog units and Traffic. The MPS is now expanding these deployments to all frontline police officers via a three-year contract to provide 22,000 BWV devices, which was awarded in late 2015.[6]

The 'tech combinations' in the connected police officer scenario may include IoT devices such as BWV cameras, environmental sensors, biomonitoring sensors and gun holster sensors, as well as wearables such as smart glasses, mobile devices of various form factors, and data analytics.

In the wearables arena, devices such as smart glasses and smart watches are particularly suited to scenarios such as understanding and navigating the physical environment, providing detailed guidance for complex manual tasks, supporting military and intelligence operations, and facilitating instant information and collaboration. We'll explore each of these scenarios in more detail in Chapter 9, 'Transforming the digital workplace', as well as looking at how wearables can be used to enhance the shopping experience for consumers.

An example of where wearables can provide the next level of hands-free process optimisation in terms of detailed guidance for complex manual tasks is within large warehouses where workers need guidance finding, picking and shipping products from inventory. In 2015, global logistics provider DHL conducted a pilot in one of their warehouses in the Netherlands using smart glasses and AR. They used the smart glasses as part of a 'vision picking' pilot and found reduced error rates in the warehouse picking process and overall efficiency improvements of up to 25 per cent.[7] In the pilot, warehouse staff were guided through the warehouse by graphics displayed on their smart glasses to speed up the picking process and reduce errors.

In terms of 'tech combinations' the DHL vision picking example utilised smart glasses, together with an AR application integrated with warehouse management software. The application replaced traditional handheld scanners and paper job orders, so it can be considered a 'mobile upgrade', in terms of the four different forms of mobile process re-design we explored in Chapter 2, moving from first generation mobile technology solution to a second generation solution.

Intelligent automation is another area of significant opportunity in transforming the digital workplace and has been the subject of considerable media attention due to its implications on future jobs. We're already seeing the convergence of human–machine work processes, where humans are becoming increasingly instrumented and machines are becoming increasingly connected with humans to create an optimised blend of human–machine participation and interaction.

Cognitive systems and intelligent automation techniques are reducing costs and dependence on labour-based processes and optimising service efficiency. Advances in machine learning, expert systems and robotics are leading to automation opportunities in both virtual (that is, software) and physical scenarios.

A relevant software-based example is the emerging role of what are known as 'cognitive virtual agents' or 'virtual engineers' in the next-generation call centre. These agents interface on human terms in natural language. They think, speak and learn on the job – improving business processes and making better-informed decisions. A recent example is IPSoft's Amelia technology, which is being used to transform the IT operations labour mix with digital labour costing one-third of the typical human FTE cost.

We'll explore strategies for transforming the digital workplace in more detail in Chapter 9. The key point again here is that various technology enablers can come together to deliver completely new opportunities to improve employee health and wellbeing, safety, collaboration and productivity, while at the same time reducing costs through automation and minimising risk through improved monitoring and management. One of the issues, of course, is that some of these scenarios may raise concerns with regard to job security and privacy, so this must be carefully considered before rushing in.

Optimising digital infrastructure and simplifying management

As the IT industry moves into the next wave of corporate IT, built upon the foundation of SMAC, the data centre of the future needs to embrace this new paradigm for the digitisation of business models and processes, with the data centre becoming the workhorse that hosts, manages and delivers this compelling new experience for end-user computing.

Today's data centres no longer reside in a small number of physical locations, but are becoming highly virtualised and highly distributed as organisations move to a hybrid IT approach that combines the best aspects of on-premise, outsourced, public and private cloud environments. This approach enables CIOs and data centre managers to place application workloads where they are most effective based on considerations related to their financial, performance and security requirements.

At the same time as the data centre needs to deliver a new generation of SMAC-enabled applications to digital consumers, and to the digital workforce, it also needs to embrace the changes occurring within data centre technologies themselves. In recent years, there have been a number of technology innovations relating to data centre operations and management that have helped to optimise data centre processes through enhanced automation, abstraction and security including:

- **Fabric computing architectures** – By adopting a fabric-based architecture, organisations can gain the agility and flexibility of shared resource pools such as compute, network and storage. This helps to avoid data centre sprawl, where each mission-critical application used to have its own dedicated physical server, and helps to speed deployments and reduce costs.

- **Software-defined principles** – By adopting software-defined principles and applying them to the management of applications, infrastructure (such as networks and storage) and even security, organisations can implement a single, software-defined management approach across all environments and eliminate the need for many time-consuming, labour-based activities such as network and firewall configuration.

- **SDDC** – The concept of software-defined principles has given rise to software defined networks (SDNs) as well as the broader concept of the SDDC, where compute, network and storage resources are all software defined.

- **Cloud management** – By adopting advanced automation tools that extend across their hybrid cloud infrastructures, organisations can reduce their operational and infrastructure costs, and selectively run workloads in the infrastructure best suited to meet their financial, performance and security requirements.

- **Security** – By adopting security technologies that focus on securing communities of interest as opposed to securing the traditional 'perimeter', organisations can change the security paradigm and take a more dynamic, software-defined approach that enhances overall manageability.

For the CIO and data centre manager, it's therefore no longer just about taking a hybrid IT approach across various deployment environments to optimise application performance, but it's also about taking advantage of the cost and agility benefits of these emerging platform and infrastructural technologies, such as converged infrastructures, fabrics, SDNs and, ultimately, SDDCs.

In terms of 'tech combinations' for their future data centres, CIOs are therefore looking at a combination of enablers consisting of those mentioned above, together with new cloud and hybrid IT, intelligent automation and cyber security technologies. The goal is to retain the mission-critical capabilities of their traditional data centres, yet expand this to support modern, digitally transformed business processes and their associated users, applications and devices.

As we saw earlier, common groupings of services can address specific business objectives and accelerate time-to-market. Rather than build out every foundational element, you may be able to find off-the-shelf capabilities where the various technology enablers have been pre-integrated and pre-packaged so you can put them to work immediately. For example, you may find a SDDC capability that has already pre-integrated the traditional SDDC components of 'compute', 'network' and 'storage' with additional elements such as software-defined security and software-defined management.

In addition to build versus buy considerations for the future data centre, CIOs also have the option of tapping into external services delivered as-a-service in the cloud. This is a growing trend for CIOs to wish to focus less on managing IT and more on innovating with the business. As a result, rather than a few physical buildings equipped with hundreds of servers, the data centre of the future will be highly distributed and highly virtualised and will tap into specific services offered by a broad array of partners and providers.

We'll explore the emerging requirements for the data centre of the future, as well as enabling technologies, strategies and executive recommendations in more detail in Chapter 11, 'Optimising digital infrastructure and simplifying management'.

Strategy considerations

When we think about these various target business objectives, ranging from enhancing the digital customer experience, to transforming the digital workplace, to optimising digital infrastructure and simplifying management, the questions and considerations are numerous:

- How should corporate innovation programmes be fine-tuned for digital transformation?
- How can you quickly identify and prioritise opportunities for digital initiatives?
- How can you time your move into a specific disruptive technology?
- What are the key elements of the digital customer experience?
- What are the future human–machine work scenarios?
- How do you optimise hand-offs between humans and machines in the future workplace?

- What digital technologies and platforms should an organisation build versus buy?
- What is the best way to jump-start transformation of the data centre?

In Parts II and III of this book, we'll address each of these questions as we deep-dive into how to lead and organise for digital transformation and how to plan your digital strategies for specific target business outcomes.

EXPLOITING THE POWER OF ECOSYSTEM BUSINESS MODELS

Just as there's a dominant technology platform for digital business, comprised of a set of foundational emerging and disruptive technologies, there's also a dominant new business model emerging in the form of digital business ecosystems. In terms of definitions around a dominant new business model, we need to look at both the definition of a 'digital ecosystem' as well as the definition of a 'digital platform'. Digital ecosystems can be defined as a network of organisations involved in the production and consumption of digital business services by way of competition and collaboration. Within this overall ecosystem, where there is competition among entities, there may also be specific ecosystem communities that have come together, by design, to compete using their collective capabilities. These digital ecosystems may be wired together in various configurations with a platform model being one instance where there is a dominant platform provider serving as the focal point for the other providers and consumers.

Platforms are defined in the book *Platform Revolution* by Parker, Van Alstyne and Choudary as follows:

> A **platform** is a business based on enabling value-creating interactions between external producers and consumers. The platform provides an open, participative infrastructure for these interactions and sets governance conditions for them. The platform's overarching purpose: to consummate matches among users and facilitate the exchange of goods, services, or social currency, thereby enabling value creation for all participants.

Digital business ecosystems and platforms are fast becoming the go-to business model for the digital economy. According to Accenture,[8] 'Ecosystems are the new bedrock of digital' and 'The top 15 public platform companies already represent $2.6 trillion in market capitalization worldwide.'

Examples of platform companies include Airbnb, Alibaba, Alphabet, Amazon, Apple, Facebook, LinkedIn, Microsoft, Netflix, Salesforce, Tencent, Twitter and Uber, among many others. All these companies have established platforms where value is exchanged between parties in the form of products, services or social currency. In addition, many, if not all, have built an ecosystem around their platform business model whereby additional ecosystem partners add to the platform's overall value proposition with primary or secondary value-added products and services.

Take, for example, Apple's iOS platform business model. The platform is centred on their iOS mobile operating system for products such as the iPhone, iPad and iPod, with value provided to end users through services directly from Apple, such as the intrinsic technology features built into their devices, as well as content and services from Apple's ecosystem of partners in the form of third-party content providers and app developers. The Apple model can therefore be considered a platform business model with an ecosystem approach generating tremendous 'network effects' in terms of value for end users and revenues for the company.

Companies from non-technology sectors are rapidly building and deploying platform business models as well. Examples include those of Bosch (Bosch Software Innovations), Disney (MagicBands), GE (Predix), Merck (Global Health Innovation) and Schneider Electric (Wonderware) to name just a few.

GE's Predix platform is an interesting example where GE offers what they term 'the world's first industrial operating system'. Predix is a cloud-based operating system and platform

> for building applications that connect to industrial assets, collect and analyze data, and deliver real-time insights for optimizing industrial infrastructure and operations.[9]

The platform offers extensive data management and analytics capabilities as well as the economics of a centrally managed and shared infrastructure in a pay-as-you-go subscription model. Some of the use cases supported by Predix include:

- scheduling and logistics;
- connected products;
- intelligent cities;
- field force management;
- industrial analytics;
- asset performance management;
- operations optimisation.

According to GE, some of the benefits of their platform model include the ability for developers to build apps quickly, leverage work elsewhere, reduce sources of error, develop and share best practices, lower risk of cost and time overruns, and future-proof their initial investments. In addition,

> independent third parties can also build apps and services on the platform, allowing businesses to extend capabilities easily by tapping the industrial ecosystem.[10]

The power of the platform: rapid scale

One of the reasons platform business models are so successful and so highly valued by the financial markets is that since they typically provide the base digital infrastructure (that is, the 'platform') and rely on external producers and consumers to provide the actual – physical or digital – products, services and social currency, they can scale up and achieve critical mass very quickly. As they grow, they also benefit from so-called 'network effects', as more participants on the platform increase the volume and variety of products, services and social currency and correspondingly increase the value proposition for all involved. This creates a virtuous cycle, which spurs further growth of the platform.

As an example, despite owning no physical assets, taxi service Uber famously reached a market capitalisation of over \$50 billion in less than five years.[11] Equally, home-rental service Airbnb has been valued at over \$25 billion,[12] despite owning no rental properties itself. This rapid scaling in capability is something that would be impossible for traditional players using traditional techniques, which require heavy investments in physical assets and infrastructure.

This leads us to an interesting point. In addition to being able to scale rapidly due to network effects as they grow, platform business models also gain rapid traction since they offer a more efficient digital business model and corresponding set of digital processes. As we saw in Chapter 2, the strategic options for digital business models include digitising products and services, to running or participating within industry platforms, to tapping into the sharing economy and crowdsourcing, to reshaping value networks, to creating new models for monetisation.

Many of the most successful platform companies are incorporating many of these elements into their models so that they're not just operating a platform, but are digitising or partially digitising the process, tapping into the sharing economy and reshaping the traditional value chain all at once. These changes allow them to deliver a highly compelling value proposition for customers where the digital customer experience has been completely re-imagined.

The power of the ecosystem: aggregating and integrating value propositions

Both consumer and industrial ecosystems are driven by customers demanding more intuitive, real-time, integrated solutions and services whether in financial services, manufacturing, transportation, health care, entertainment, the public sector or any other industry vertical.

By addressing a continuum of needs along the customer journey, companies operating as part of a business ecosystem can expand their addressable market and simultaneously deliver greater value in terms of the digital customer experience and overall value proposition.

In the world of digital business ecosystems, you may no longer be playing solely in your traditional markets. Organisations need to think about the end-to-end customer journey in specific scenarios and the discrete value propositions that can be aggregated together via the ecosystem or platform.

In air travel, this might involve thinking about the overall passenger experience that cuts across airlines, airports, car rental agencies and hotels. In the automotive world, this might involve thinking about the future of self-driving cars and implications on roadside service, insurance and other traditional services that can be re-imagined and re-designed.

As an example, the RAC is the UK's leading motoring services company. Its recent acquisition of vehicle diagnostics specialists Nebula Systems[13] shows it's thinking about next-generation services for motorists that extends its business model from a reactive, labour-based model to a more pro-active, digitally enabled 'predictive breakdown service'. By acquiring and partnering with high-tech companies, the RAC is enhancing its ecosystem to react to the evolving needs of its members.

Strategy considerations

According to Ralph Welborn, CEO at Imaginatik, an innovation management software provider,

> Business ecosystems are no aberration; nor are they a surprise. They represent an inevitable, adaptive response to changes in the types of value that folks care about and the interplay of technology innovation, behavioural expectations, regulatory changes and novel business models.[14]

By 2018, IDC predicts that more than 50 per cent of large enterprises – and more than 80 per cent of enterprises with advanced digital transformation strategies – 'will create and/or partner with industry platforms'.[15] All this leads to a number of important considerations in terms of how organisations need to think about strategy and innovation in the years ahead.

On the business strategy side, the questions and considerations are numerous:

- What percentage of investment should go into ecosystem business models?
- What types of ecosystems should be considered?
- When should an organisation choose a hub versus spoke strategy?
- What is an appropriate pricing strategy that will spur growth of the ecosystem or platform?
- Should an organisation hedge its bets by playing within competing ecosystems?
- What sustainable competitive advantage and differentiation can be gained from an ecosystem model versus a traditional value chain-oriented business model?

The implications on strategy and execution also ripple back to corporate innovation. Just as corporate strategic planning will need to respond to the new environment (that is, the growing ecosystem and platform economy), so too will corporate innovation programmes.

On the IT strategy side, the questions and considerations are equally numerous:

- What's the right value proposition to attract developers to the platform?
- What open standards, APIs and other technical capabilities are required for ease of onboarding?
- What key infrastructural services should be provided?
- What cloud platforms can scale sufficiently as the number of participants grows?

- Where should data reside in light of geographic and legal considerations?
- What security model will best support the platform model and full set of participants?

The early signs are that most players in the platform economy are starting with a robust and scalable cloud platform, incorporating open standards and APIs to aid with onboarding and integration of developers and partners, incorporating governance to establish the operating rules for the platform, and then adding in data management and analytics services to provide value-added services for participants.

For organisations in non-technology sectors, all of this can be more difficult than it may initially appear. Companies such as Microsoft and Apple made onboarding for their third-party developers very easy with a wealth of training, education, developer kits and APIs. According to Peter C. Evans, Vice President, The Center for Global Enterprise, there are some large differences between consumer-facing and industrial platforms. Apps can be tricky to deploy, due to complexity and data compatibility issues. In addition, developers themselves can be tricky to onboard, due to the less attractive nature of industrial applications and the requirement for deeper domain expertise.

To explore the challenges and opportunities presented by industrial platforms further, in our case study below we take an in-depth look at the broad set of requirements spelled out by the Industry 4.0 Working Group for the German vision for the future of manufacturing. While Industry 4.0 is still a futuristic vision, it helps to show the end game that many platform business models are aiming towards in terms of digitally transforming their entire industries.

CASE STUDY – INDUSTRY 4.0

Building on the new platform for digital business

When exploring digital business ecosystems and platforms, Industry 4.0 (aka Industrie 4.0) – the German vision for the future of manufacturing – is an interesting example because it taps into a broad array of foundational technologies as well as a broad array of smart factories, smart products and 'the Internet of Things, People and Services' across its ecosystem.

When thinking about the Industrial Internet and Industry 4.0, one tends to gravitate towards the IoT, and perhaps data analytics, as the key underlying technologies. However, more than just the IoT and big data/fast data/data analytics, the real potential of the Industrial Internet and Industry 4.0 will be realised by the holistic combination of a far broader set of technology enablers to deliver 'dynamic, real-time optimized, self-organizing value chains'.

The vision articulated by the Industrie 4.0 Working Group in their 'Recommendations for implementing the strategic initiative INDUSTRIE 4.0' is a useful example to see how these elements all come together in a powerful combination to enable the fourth industrial revolution.[16]

Vision of Industry 4.0

'Industry 4.0' was coined by representatives from German industry, research, industrial associations and industrial unions. The number 4.0 refers to the fourth industrial revolution – the theme of the 2016 annual general meeting of the World Economic Forum – and is represented by cyber-physical production systems (CPS) that combine communications, IT, data and physical elements in collaborative inter-company ecosystems. Industry 4.0 specifically focuses on manufacturing, whereas the Industrial Internet is of course focused on a broader range of industries.

The vision of Industry 4.0 is to deliver 'greater flexibility and robustness together with the highest quality standards in engineering, planning, manufacturing, operational, and logistics processes'. The idea is that customers benefit from faster innovation cycles and individualised mass production (that is, 'lot size of 1'), and manufacturers can shorten time-to-market and optimise and change their processes with ease.

Companies digitising their manufacturing processes expect to increase flexibility and responsiveness, improve quality and reduce defects, and increase efficiency and reduce costs. In fact, a study on Industry 4.0 by PwC indicates that manufacturers expect to achieve up to 18% in increased efficiency and 14% in cost savings by 2020.[17]

Foundational technologies

A key aspect of the technology vision behind Industry 4.0 is that it incorporates far more than just IoT components and big data analytics. In fact, it draws on the same set of foundational technologies that you'll see in many next-generation blueprints for digital business platforms as per our earlier model.

Some of the key elements include personas and context, social business, mobility and wearables, big data analytics, cloud and hybrid IT, intelligent automation, IoT and cyber security, as shown in Figure 4.1. In the illustration, I've shown our model for the new platform for digital business and have highlighted the key requirements for Industry 4.0 – as specified in the Industrie 4.0 Working Group recommendations – alongside. The Industry 4.0 vision clearly taps into all these foundational technologies and more.

Ecosystem approach

The ultimate goal from a manufacturing standpoint is to enable continuous resource productivity and efficiency gains to be delivered across the entire value network (that is, ecosystem), incorporating smart factories and smart products, as well as the IoT, people and services.

According to the Working Group, smart factories are

> embedded into inter-company value networks and characterized by end-to-end engineering that encompasses both the manufacturing process and the manufactured product.

Figure 4.1 Industry 4.0 requirements mapped to the new platform for digital business

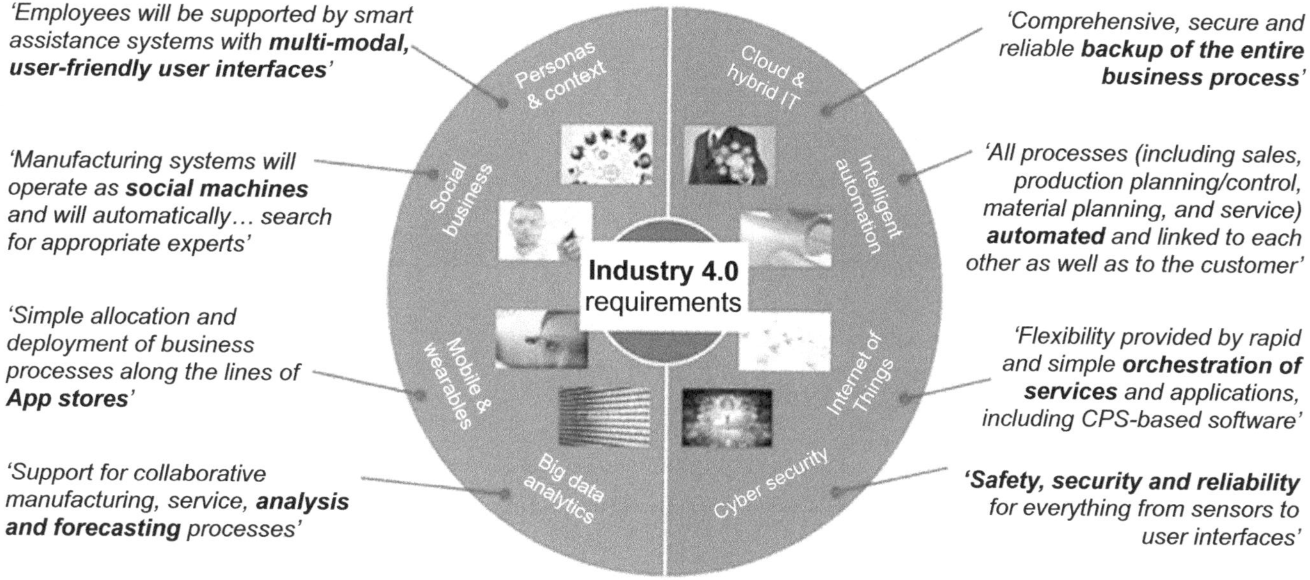

'Comprehensive, secure and reliable *backup of the entire business process*'

'All processes (including sales, production planning/control, material planning, and service) *automated* and linked to each other as well as to the customer'

'Flexibility provided by rapid and simple *orchestration of services* and applications, including CPS-based software'

'*Safety, security and reliability* for everything from sensors to user interfaces'

'Employees will be supported by smart assistance systems with *multi-modal, user-friendly user interfaces*'

'Manufacturing systems will operate as *social machines* and will automatically... search for appropriate experts'

'Simple allocation and deployment of business processes along the lines of *App stores*'

'Support for collaborative manufacturing, service, *analysis and forecasting* processes'

Intelligent automation

Internet of Things

Cloud & hybrid IT

Cyber security

Industry 4.0 requirements

Personas & context

Social business

Mobile & wearables

Big data analytics

Smart products are

> uniquely identifiable and locatable at all times. Even while they are being made, they know the details of their own manufacturing process.

One of the key takeaways here is that while the IoT constitutes a complex ecosystem in and of itself, the full vision of Industry 4.0, and by extension the Industrial Internet, will incorporate an even broader ecosystem of technology enablers and industry participants.

More than IoT sensors, devices, gateways, middleware, applications and data, it's important to design for the next evolution of human–machine collaboration and to work in the appropriate technology enablers related to personas and context, social collaboration and mobile applications to enable 'unprecedented communications between parts to be created, other components, companies, and end users' in this highly distributed model.

As the Industry 4.0 working group puts it, the vision will be characterised by a 'new level of socio-technical interaction between all the actors and resources involved in manufacturing'.

With the broad scope of Industry 4.0, within the logical architecture, there will be many different organisations and partners each providing specific products and services. This will need to include the integration of applications and systems that span the factory floor, controls and automation, manufacturing execution systems and enterprise resource planning as well as a robust base layer of horizontal capabilities such as information and communications technology (ICT) infrastructure, cloud technology and services, big data analytics, mobile technologies and security, among others.

Challenges and opportunities

Many challenges lie ahead, including sizeable hurdles related to security as well as interoperability. Organisations such as the Industrial Internet Consortium[18] are helping to tackle these challenges via their reference architectures and test beds, and this will help to accelerate market momentum.

As these initial barriers to adoption start to become addressed, and with a solid vision and blueprint for the requisite technology enablers to help shape the 'big picture', the next step for enterprise organisations wishing to move to the vision of Industry 4.0 and the Industrial Internet will be mapping out a strategic roadmap for transformation.

The opportunities for those organisations who either lead or embed themselves within the new industry ecosystems will be as profound and rewarding as they were for the organisations who made similar transitions into the first, second and third industrial revolutions related to mechanisation, mass production, and computers and automation respectively.

KEY TAKEAWAYS FOR CHAPTER 4

- While SMAC capabilities are now expected by default in leading consumer applications, the new competitive battleground will be fought with new weaponry that taps into the power of personas and context, wearables and AR, the IoT and intelligent automation.

- Just as there's a dominant technology platform for digital business, comprised of a set of foundational emerging and disruptive technologies, there's also a dominant new business model emerging in the form of digital business ecosystems.

- By addressing a continuum of needs along the customer journey, companies operating as part of a business ecosystem can expand their addressable market and simultaneously deliver greater value in terms of the digital customer experience and overall value proposition.

- It is the mix of disruptive technologies and platform business models, together with a mastery of digital services – in terms of how digital services are designed, developed, deployed, managed and continually evolved – that really sets today's digital business leaders head and shoulders above the rest of the field. These elements are therefore at the heart of truly mastering digital business and crafting a successful strategy and roadmap for the years ahead.

- While the IoT constitutes a complex ecosystem in and of itself, the full vision of Industry 4.0, and by extension the Industrial Internet, will incorporate an even broader ecosystem of technology enablers and industry participants.

- The opportunities for organisations who either lead or embed themselves within new industry ecosystems, such as the Industrial Internet, will be as profound and rewarding as they were for the organisations who made similar transitions into the first, second and third industrial revolutions related to mechanisation, mass production, and computers and automation.

PART II
PLANNING – LEADING AND ORGANISING FOR DIGITAL TRANSFORMATION

5 ORGANISING AND ADAPTING CORPORATE INNOVATION PROCESSES FOR DIGITAL TRANSFORMATION

Innovation distinguishes between a leader and a follower.

Steve Jobs[1]

In one form or another, most organisations have had a corporate innovation programme for many years now. Today's innovation objectives, however, are all gravitating towards digital transformation. This chapter provides leadership guidance on how to change and fine-tune an existing corporate innovation programme to most effectively support digital transformation both now and in the years to come.

THE FIVE CRITICAL PILLARS OF INNOVATION MANAGEMENT CAPABILITY

Before we look at how to change and fine-tune an existing corporate innovation programme to set the sights squarely around digital transformation, it's worth looking at the five critical pillars of corporate innovation management to help frame our understanding of the key capabilities a corporate innovation programme should provide.

While idea management is often the first item to come to mind when thinking about innovation, it's actually just the tip of the iceberg. Corporate innovation programmes need to go beyond the table-stakes of idea management and provide a complete programme addressing not only the innovation pipeline (that is, idea management), but the front-end of the innovation lifecycle in terms of 'where to play' and the back-end of the lifecycle in terms of 'how to scale'. This is where innovation needs to be closely aligned with strategy and execution.

Just like any other corporate programme, the key elements need to address strategy and intent, people, process and technology. Your innovation programme should also address the highly interrelated internal and external aspects of managing innovation and extend across employees, partners and customers.

Figure 5.1 shows the five critical pillars of innovation management capability that I believe need to be a part of any major initiative within mid-size to large organisations:

- Innovation management and measurement.
- Innovation infrastructure.
- Internal innovation community.

- Open innovation community.
- Customer innovation community.

Figure 5.1 The five critical pillars of innovation management capability

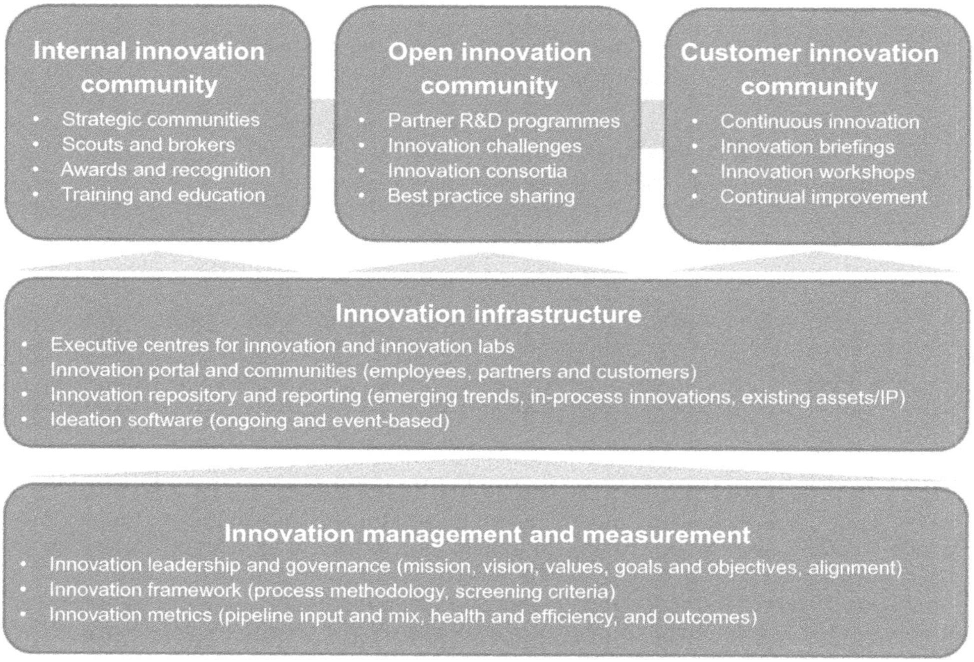

Internal innovation community
- Strategic communities
- Scouts and brokers
- Awards and recognition
- Training and education

Open innovation community
- Partner R&D programmes
- Innovation challenges
- Innovation consortia
- Best practice sharing

Customer innovation community
- Continuous innovation
- Innovation briefings
- Innovation workshops
- Continual improvement

Innovation infrastructure
- Executive centres for innovation and innovation labs
- Innovation portal and communities (employees, partners and customers)
- Innovation repository and reporting (emerging trends, in-process innovations, existing assets/IP)
- Ideation software (ongoing and event-based)

Innovation management and measurement
- Innovation leadership and governance (mission, vision, values, goals and objectives, alignment)
- Innovation framework (process methodology, screening criteria)
- Innovation metrics (pipeline input and mix, health and efficiency, and outcomes)

Here's an in-depth look at each of these areas.

1. Innovation management and measurement

Key elements: innovation leadership and governance | innovation processes | innovation metrics and analytics

This is the strategy and intent portion of your innovation management approach that includes overall leadership and governance, innovation processes, and innovation metrics and analytics. According to David Sanders,[2] founder of Dallas Advisory Partners, the top three ingredients for success that need to be in place from the beginning are executive leadership, enterprise programme management and change management. These are essential elements not just for corporate innovation programmes, but for any kind of transformational initiative.

Core processes should include innovation frameworks (that is, process methodologies) for identifying, prioritising, incubating and commercialising innovative solutions and offerings, as well as measuring, monitoring and reporting on innovation metrics.

The innovation process methodology should support what I term 'multi-modal idea-tion' (that is, multi-modal idea generation) in terms of both event-based and ongoing ideation:

- **Event-based ideation (idea generation)** – This ranges from large-scale, innovation events such as single- or multi-day, corporate-wide 'innovation jams', to innovation contests and partnerships with innovation labs, to laser-focused innovation workshops with a select group of subject matter experts (SMEs).

- **Ongoing ideation (idea generation)** – This ranges from corporate-wide suggestion boxes and innovation databases of various levels of sophistication, to more focused ideation processes typically aligned with corporate strategic communities, or corporate strategic planning cycles.

By supporting both event-based and ongoing ideation, your organisation will be well-poised to maximise the innovation potential across your diverse ecosystem of employees, customers, suppliers and partners in a systematic manner and equally able to mobilise high-targeted ideation sessions as, where and when opportunities arise.

In terms of metrics, there are literally hundreds of innovation metrics that can be meas-ured by the typical organisation. By performing factor analysis on these metrics, it has been recognised by groups such as the Corporate Executive Board[3] that they all come down to three basic areas of measurement:

- **Innovation input and mix** – What's going into your innovation pipeline in terms of the types of innovations in the queue.

- **Innovation health and efficiency** – The flow-rate through your pipeline and the amount of funding being applied.

- **Innovation outcomes** – The measure of your return on innovation in terms of the number of innovations that have made it through to commercialisation and have captured revenues or other strategic or financial objectives.

2. Innovation infrastructure

Key elements: innovation centres and labs | innovation portal and communities | innovation repositories and reporting | idea management software

This is the physical infrastructure and technology portion of your innovation manage-ment approach that may include physical centres of excellence and innovation labs as well as software tools such as innovation portals, to support communication and collaboration among your various communities, together with innovation databases (that is, repositories) to support your process methodology for innovation.

An innovation database can serve as the centralised repository to support the innova-tion framework process and from which to draw reports and metrics that can be further analysed via an innovation dashboard. One of the key upfront requirements for any inno-vation database is to define the scope of what's included very carefully and to educate employees on the range of usage scenarios.

An innovation database is typically the core idea management system for the organisation, helping you collect, manage and prioritise ideas, but it can also be extended to provide a broader view of future solutions for the organisation as well as a view of existing innovative assets and capabilities.

A more extensive innovation database may therefore include:

1. Emerging trends and technologies that are on the radar.
2. Future solutions, offerings and ideas that constitute the next wave of solutions.
3. Existing assets and capabilities that have the potential for reuse across the organisation.

A key consideration within this pillar is to continually innovate around the use of the technologies themselves and incorporate newer elements such as 'gamification' (that is, the application of game-design elements and game principles) and advanced analytics to further fuel innovation activities and lend additional insights.

While most innovation management software on the market today includes social and mobile features to assist with idea management via crowdsourcing and anytime, anywhere access, it's important to look beyond these relatively commonplace features and look for more advanced capabilities that can help you to process large numbers of ideas in the most efficient manner.

3. Internal innovation community

Key elements: strategic communities | scouts and brokers | awards and recognition | training and education

This is the employee-facing portion of your innovation management approach that includes elements such as innovation councils, innovation communities of practice, scouts and brokers, award and recognition schemes, employee communications and training, and employee feedback mechanisms.

Basically, scouts and brokers are formally assigned resources who search for opportunities and then direct them to the appropriate parts of the organisation. To get everyone on the same page across your organisation, since 'innovation' typically means different things to different people, it's important to come up with precise terminology for innovation and to clearly spell out initiatives, roles and responsibilities to avoid duplication of effort or competition among internal groups.

This programme area is vital to achieving corporate goals of institutionalising innovation within the organisation and making innovation part of corporate DNA. As such, it requires continual care and feeding in order to engage employees and build success in step with the innovation maturity of the organisation. Employee communications and training are also vital ongoing tasks, which must be maintained and promoted year-over-year to preserve organisational memory, to train new hires as they come on board, and to share and build upon success.

4. Open innovation community

Key elements: partner research and development (R&D) programmes | innovation challenges | innovation consortia | best practice sharing

This is the external-facing portion of your innovation management approach that includes industry-recognised approaches such as open innovation and crowdsourcing for bringing in ideas from the outside, together with collaboration in various innovation consortia for best practice sharing.

Depending on your particular industry and organisation, this collaboration with customers and partners may constitute a large percentage of your sources of innovation and may be a central part of your innovation strategy.

A good example of this is P&G's 'Connect + Develop' program.[4] Through their open innovation strategy, P&G has established more than 2,000 successful agreements with innovation partners around the world. Through their website, www.pgconnectdevelop.com/, P&G enables current and potential partners to submit their ideas to P&G by, first, reviewing their innovation needs list, reviewing their criteria for submitting ideas, and then submitting their ideas related to innovative technologies, ready to go products or packaging, or commercial opportunities 'that can help improve the lives of consumers around the world'.

Other activities within this programme area may include alliance partner R&D programmes, where organisations collaborate and work with alliance partners further upstream so they can gain insights into the innovations that are on the radars of their partners and co-create future solutions.

5. Customer innovation community

Key elements: continuous innovation | innovation briefings | innovation workshops | continual improvement

This is the customer-facing portion of your innovation management approach that includes all programme elements and activities that you make available to your customers. This may include co-innovation with customers on a continual basis, via mechanisms such as innovation councils, innovation briefings and innovation workshops, as well as innovation research via customer focus groups and feedback mechanisms.

Continual and collaborative innovation with customers can help infuse innovation in two fundamental areas. The first is innovation within the current scope of your company's products and services, and the second is in helping them with innovation above and beyond the current scope of your relationship.

If your customers are a major source of much of your product or service innovation, then this pillar may well be closely aligned with, or even an integral part of, the open innovation community pillar.

If your external sources of innovation come mostly from partners, then you may find that two distinct pillars are beneficial so that you can manage and fine-tune each programme area specifically for those constituents.

However you organise, it's likely that open innovation will be a common approach across all three 'people' pillars.

Leading and organising across the five pillars

Overall, it's important to manage across all five of these critical pillars of innovation management capability and to ensure they all connect into the appropriate corporate strategy, investment and product, and service development processes.

According to Steve Hill,[5] Global Head of Innovation and Investments at KPMG, the three people-oriented pillars are the most challenging yet most important part of driving an innovation management capability. It takes leadership to make innovation a necessity, to enforce behaviours, and to keep programmes chartered and aligned with the external perspective in mind.

In organising for innovation, Ralph Welborn,[6] CEO at Imaginatik, an innovation management software provider, believes it is also important to ask what he believes is the 'new strategic question' of today – namely, where value is being created and destroyed within your ecosystem and, consequently, how to orchestrate your capabilities to respond.

By taking a programmatic and holistic approach you can ensure that your innovation programme covers all strategic angles and can support and sustain innovation and contribute to both your top and bottom lines. You'll be able to engage in continual and collaborative innovation with customers, expand your sources of innovation, and accelerate their commercialisation into new products and services or differentiators for existing offerings.

ADAPTING INNOVATION PROGRAMMES FOR DIGITAL TRANSFORMATION

As companies pursue digital transformation initiatives, one of the strategic questions that often arises relates to the organisational model for programmatically managing these initiatives from strategy to execution.

While it's well recognised that digital transformation initiatives have to be a team sport, with sponsorship, involvement and collaboration of many key stakeholders from the CEO to the CMO, Chief Digital Officer (CDO) and Chief Technology Officer (CTO), another key consideration is the role of corporate innovation programmes.

In one form or another, most organisations have had a corporate innovation programme for many years. Today's innovation objectives, however, are all gravitating towards digital transformation. So how should an existing corporate innovation programme change or be fine-tuned to most effectively support digital transformation both now and in the years to come?

Figure 5.2 presents five key points, which I hope will provide some useful considerations and guidance.

Figure 5.2 Key aspects of a finely tuned innovation programme supporting digital transformation

1. First, regardless of how it's organised, the innovation programme should deliver the transformative outcomes required of digital business

In some companies, such as many start-ups and well-recognised high-tech 'innovators', innovation is a core part of their corporate DNA and is simply embedded in the business. It's viral across the organisation and a part of 'business as usual'. Other organisations, particularly larger enterprises, often accelerate innovation by way of a structured programme. The various options include:

- Specialised departments (e.g. traditional R&D departments, incubators and corporate venture groups).

- The formation of dedicated business units around distinct growth horizons (for example, the three horizons framework featured in *The alchemy of growth*).[7]

- Creating hybrid models where innovation is collaboratively managed by multiple departments.

According to Steve Hill,[8] there are two key areas to organise around innovation: one is embedded in the business and the other is distinct and protected from the business. In the first area, incremental innovation should occur within the business and support the kind of viral innovation that does not need heavy, top-down involvement. In the second area, disruptive innovation should be distinct from the business and have the protection and centralised funding it needs to succeed.

The general idea is to carve out distinct business units or departments to focus on more disruptive opportunities and investments and to avoid *The innovator's dilemma*.[9] Basically,

> successful companies can put too much emphasis on customers' current needs, and fail to adopt new technology or business models that will meet customers' unstated or future needs.

For both of these models, it's important that the programmes deliver on the business outcomes they aim to realise. It's therefore worth re-visiting the measurements and metrics around your innovation programme, and adjusting where necessary. As we saw earlier, a common approach to innovation metrics, based on extensive analysis by the Corporate Executive Board, is the pipeline model where you look at the pipeline mix (in terms of the sources, categories, quality and quantity of ideas flowing into the pipeline), the pipeline productivity and health (the flow-rate in terms of duration from initial idea to commercialisation, and the amount of funding provided) and the business outcomes (in terms of increased revenues, reduced costs, increased customer satisfaction and so on).

In the era of digital business, you may want to accelerate (that is, shorten) your average cycle time for commercialisation or operationalisation and also change the relative mix of what goes into the pipeline, what gets commercialised and how you measure it. According to Steve Hill, the cycles of innovation are very different today and organisations can't buy time at the expense of their long-term sustainability.

2. The innovation programme should adjust for the scope of digital transformation initiatives

The corporate innovation programme should contribute to delivering the desired business outcomes related to digital transformation. This means its focus may need to be adjusted in terms of the degree of innovation (that is, disruptive versus incremental) and the type of innovation (that is, business model, process, products, services and so on).

It's likely that your innovation programme already takes a holistic view across all these areas, so the change needed may just be in terms of relative priorities. For example, if your existing programme places equal emphasis on identifying and incubating highly disruptive ideas as well as more incremental ideas that can benefit your business, then you may just need to amplify the focus on the former.

So, precisely what's the right mix of disruptive versus incremental innovation to support digital transformation initiatives? According to Steve Hill, there's no ideal mix since it will vary considerably from company to company and where they are in the 'invest', 'sustain' and 'harvest' cycle within their business strategy. However, this is an interesting area for board member discussions since it takes the innovation strategy of a company beyond the typical 'innovate/maintain' investment mix discussion into specifics related to their more disruptive and transformative investments.

3. The innovation programme should be driven by what's important to customers

Since the majority of digital transformation initiatives are focused on re-thinking and re-inventing business models and processes to improve the digital customer experience, it's important that the innovation programme is driven by what's impactful to customers.

There are many ways to accomplish this alignment, ranging all the way from customer-facing innovation workshops for collaborative innovation with your customers and prospects, to how you score and prioritise your innovation initiatives, to how you continually adjust your programme based on customer feedback.

What I've found in conducting hundreds of innovation workshops over the years is that customers are typically interested in two fundamental areas of innovation. The first is innovation within the current scope of your company's products and services, and the second is in helping them with innovation above and beyond the current scope of your relationship.

They're often interested in how your company can help them outside your current scope of work. What additional innovative ideas can you bring to the table to help them in their business? If your company is a business-to-consumer (B2C) operation, then the equivalent question your customers may be asking is what else can you bring to them beyond your current product or service offerings. Going back to the innovator's dilemma, they're basically asking you about their unstated and future needs and providing a green light for you to collaborate with them.

4. Ensure strong connections and innovation leadership within the business

Growth horizons for an organisation are usually described as horizon 1 (core products and services typically comprising 70 per cent of the company's annual investment), horizon 2 (emerging businesses and adjacencies typically comprising 20 per cent of the company's annual investment) and horizon 3 (new, transformational initiatives and 'viable options' typically comprising 10 per cent of the company's annual investment).

As your latest product or service innovations gain traction in the market and mature over time, they often move from horizon 3 – where they're initially incubated – to horizon 2, and then horizon 1 where they become a mainstream source of revenue for the organisation. This may well involve a transition of these innovations from your innovation centres or 'skunkworks' into the core parts of the business.

According to Steve Hill, as you transition these innovations to the business, it's important to know your innovation leaders. You need to know who's in the business, whether or not they're pre-disposed to be innovative and if it's in their job description and performance objectives. If all the above are in place, you can then measure the business, and its leaders, in terms of their ability to drive innovation.

A recent study from the Corporate Executive Board, confirms Mr Hill's position. It found that leadership quality impacts innovation potential. In fact, it found that staff of effective managers had a 34 per cent higher 'innovation potential' score on average, and that most companies' performance management systems did not identify or reward the competencies that had the largest impact on innovation potential: namely 'risk taker', 'customer empathiser', 'idea integrator', 'influencer' and 'results seeker'.

5. The innovation programme itself should be digitally transformed

Finally, the innovation programme itself should be digitally transformed. Just like any long-term initiative within an organisation, it needs to continually evolve and adapt to meet the needs of the business at any specific time. Elements of your innovation programme may come and go year-over-year, based on their level of adoption and benefits realised by the corporation. Some examples are elements such as innovation portals, databases, communities, scouts and brokers and so on. You can expect these to constantly evolve and adapt.

The elements that have the best longevity are typically those that are designed to allow for intrinsic customisation. As an example, innovation workshops that have a method-ology and toolset designed to allow for a high degree of customisation in terms of the key focus areas for each workshop can easily support a wide range of workshop topics and objectives over time.

While the content of the innovation ideas that flow through each workshop may be very different, the design principle should be such that the structured approach and toolset within the workshop methodology can be consistent and provide the necessary levels of quality, consistency and repeatability.

To digitally transform your innovation programme, you can apply the same thinking that you apply to your externally focused innovation activities. For example, think about how the SMAC stack can enable stronger social collaboration, mobile access, improved analytics and cost-effective and agile cloud delivery. Think about how innovation pro-cesses can be re-designed to be more customer facing and produce results within faster cycle times.

Adapting your innovation programme

Taken as a whole, you'll see that the innovation programme should be re-visited in light of your digital transformation objectives in terms of how it's measured, what types of innovation you focus on and their relative priorities, where and when you create key touch points with your customers, which business unit leaders you collaborate with to drive innovation and, finally, how you apply technology to transform your programme's capabilities. By assessing and then fine-tuning all these variables, you'll be able to maximise your digital business outcomes in the years ahead.

KEY TAKEAWAYS FOR CHAPTER 5

- Corporate innovation programmes need to go beyond the table-stakes of idea management and provide a complete programme addressing not only the innovation pipeline (that is, idea management), but the front-end of the innovation lifecycle in terms of 'where to play' and the back-end of the lifecycle in terms of 'how to scale'. This is where innovation needs to be closely aligned with strategy and execution.

- The five critical pillars of innovation management capability include innovation management and measurement, innovation infrastructure, internal innovation community, open innovation community, and customer innovation community.

- The three people-oriented pillars are the most challenging yet most important part of driving an innovation management capability. It takes leadership to make innovation a necessity, to enforce behaviours, and to keep programmes chartered and aligned with the external perspective in mind.

- Innovation programmes should be re-visited in light of your digital transformation objectives in terms of how they are measured, what types of innovation you focus on and their relative priorities, where and when you create key touch points with your customers, which business unit leaders you collaborate with to drive innovation, and finally how you apply technology to transform your programme's capabilities.

6 IDENTIFYING AND PRIORITISING OPPORTUNITIES WITH INNOVATION WORKSHOPS

Software innovation, like almost every other kind of innovation, requires the ability to collaborate and share ideas with other people, and to sit down and talk with customers and get their feedback and understand their needs.

Bill Gates[1]

Innovation workshops provide a way for leaders to focus on innovation opportunity identification, categorisation, prioritisation and then the development of high-level business cases and implementation roadmaps for the most promising opportunities identified. In this chapter, we'll explore the importance of both event-based and ongoing ideation – something we term 'multi-modal ideation' – and share the details of the five-step Innovation Workshop methodology together with a set of best practices for running lean, high-performance sessions. The Innovation Workshop methodology, which we'll explore, has been developed and refined over literally hundreds of innovation sessions with major corporations and government organisations worldwide. It can be utilised as a vital tool for identifying and prioritising digital business initiatives and gaining consensus across key stakeholders.

SETTING THE RHYTHM OF DIGITAL INNOVATION: EVENT-BASED AND ONGOING IDEATION

While ideation is a small part of an enterprise innovation programme, there's many things to consider in terms of targeting your ideation activities to support both the tactical and strategic needs of the business as it relates to digital transformation.

In terms of ideation tools and approaches, there's certainly no shortage of options to choose from – ranging from enterprise software, to consultancies, to problem-solver networks, to innovation contests, to partnerships with innovation labs and start-ups, to open innovation with customers and partners and so on. As we saw earlier in Chapter 5, the key consideration is that you'll likely need a combination of both event-based ideation, as well as ongoing, enterprise-wide ideation processes as part of your overall innovation strategy:

- **Event-based ideation** – This ranges from large-scale, innovation events such as single- or multi-day, corporate-wide 'innovation jams', to innovation contests and partnerships with innovation labs, to laser-focused innovation workshops with a select group of subject matter experts SMEs.

- **Ongoing ideation** – This ranges from corporate-wide suggestion boxes and innovation databases of various levels of sophistication, to more focused ideation processes typically aligned with corporate strategic communities, or corporate strategic planning cycles.

As you prepare to run a variety of ideation events and campaigns to generate digital business-related ideas and opportunities, a best practice to maximise results is to think about the pillars of strategy and intent, people, process, technology and continuous improvement as follows.

Strategy and intent

Whether event-based or ongoing ideation, it's important to ensure your ideation activities are complementary and suited to the task. Set clear goals and objectives and define your focus. A common understanding and precise definition of terms in your innovation vocabulary is essential. In addition, it's important to have a common understanding about the types of innovation that are of interest – that is, business model, business process, technology – and also the level of innovation that's of interest – that is, more incremental, tactical ideas or more disruptive, strategic ideas.

Depending on your goals and objectives, you may want to focus more on one level of innovation or the other. It's also perfectly fine to focus on both areas within an ideation session, since in many cases the goal is to come up with a set of ideas that can provide measurable business value regardless of whether they're near-term tactical opportunities or longer-term, more strategic opportunities.

People

When preparing an ideation session, it's key to target the right audience in terms of participants. Is this a shotgun approach where you're looking for general ideas from a large crowd, or more of a rifle shot where you're looking for specific ideas from specific SMEs? Often, the key focus areas for your ideation session can help to drive the selection of the appropriate internal or external SMEs.

In our innovation workshops, we've found that five to ten key focus areas (that is, categories for brainstorming) help to define the scope of the workshop and help to drive the selection of SMEs with the appropriate domain knowledge. This selection of the key focus areas is typically done well in advance of the session with the client or relevant stakeholder.

For an Innovation Workshop focused on game-changing opportunities related to digital business, some typical key focus areas might be as follows:

- enhancing the digital customer experience;
- transforming the digital workplace;
- gaining insights from analytics;
- optimising infrastructure;
- simplifying management.

The key focus areas can be any business-, process- or technology-related categories where you want to capture innovative ideas and opportunities.

Process

It's important to realise that ideation is just the first step. Ensure that there are owners taking the ideas to the next stage in terms of further exploration, screening, filtering, prioritisation and ultimate execution. The role of a facilitator running an Innovation Workshop or session should go far beyond simply facilitating the group and guiding them through an ideation session; it should also include responsibility for working with the appropriate stakeholders and individuals after the event to ensure that the ideas identified and prioritised at the session can be used to drive strategic outcomes for the business (see Figure 6.1).

Figure 6.1 The strategic role of Innovation Workshop facilitators

If your particular facilitator's scope is narrower, or if you're working with external facilitators, then ensure the appropriate hand-offs take place and there's a suitable owner post-session who's on point to carry the most promising ideas forward.

Technology

While it's always in vogue for some to downplay the role of technology, the fact is that emerging technologies are providing a foundational platform for next-generation business models, processes, products and services. We saw this back in 2015 when perhaps for the first time ever, according to the 18th PwC CEO Survey,[2] the top transformation trends from CEOs all related directly back to IT.

As we discussed in Chapter 5, the innovation programme itself should be digitally transformed as well. For example, think about how the SMAC stack can enable stronger social collaboration, mobile access, improved analytics and cost-effective and agile cloud delivery. Think about how innovation processes can be re-designed to be more customer facing and produce results within faster cycle times.

Continual improvement

Build in a continual improvement process and capture best practices learned as a result of your innovation events and processes. Best practices can span the gamut from pre-workshop planning, to the actual conduct of the workshop, to post-workshop deliverables and follow-on. After running many sessions, you'll find you know exactly how long various forms of ideation sessions may take and even how many ideas you expect to collect based on the structure of the session and the number of attendees.

While the goal is typically the quality of ideas and not the quantity, having an estimate of the number of ideas anticipated can still be highly beneficial since it will inform you of how long you may need to allocate to any subsequent steps such as voting. For continual improvement, it's also important to measure, but to measure the right elements and not everything imaginable around your ideation processes. Measure only what will be useful to understand and act upon in the future.

Finally, you may remember the movie, *Groundhog Day*, where Bill Murray wakes up day after day to the same day on 2 February until he changes his behaviour. To avoid your own 'innovation groundhog day', training and education should be a continual, available capability so that as roles change and new hires come into your organisation, they can quickly get up to speed and understand the corporate innovation vocabulary and the range of options available to them in support of their innovation objectives.

By implementing a multi-modal ideation approach, with both event-based and ongoing ideation vehicles, your organisation will be well poised to maximise the innovation potential across your diverse ecosystem of employees, customers, suppliers and partners in a systematic manner, and equally able to mobilise ideation sessions as, where and when opportunities arise.

PLANNING YOUR INNOVATION WORKSHOP

In recent years, IT has learned how to programmatically tap into creative ideas, not just for its own internal purposes, but for the overall benefit to the business. More and more, innovative ideas are a key way for companies to seek competitive advantage in a market where a steady pipeline of ideas, the ability to execute, and a 'fail fast and move on' approach is the business necessity.

When it comes to enterprise software to help manage innovation processes, there's certainly no shortage of options on the market, from idea management and crowdsourcing platforms, to innovation process management software, to open innovation software, to innovation marketplaces.

These platforms are mostly focused on enterprise-wide initiatives and are intended to operate as part of an ongoing, programmatic effort within the organisation. Of course many of them can be, and often are, applied for event-based or time-based sessions such as workshops and innovation challenges of one form or another, or even for sourcing highly targeted innovation needs, but their typical purpose is to support the ongoing execution of an enterprise innovation programme.

One area I find that complements this ongoing, enterprise-wide approach very nicely is the conduct of one- or two-day targeted innovation workshops using web-based group decision support software (GDSS). The meetings are typically conducted primarily in person with a group of 10 to 25 individuals. We use the GDSS to rapidly collect a set of ideas and innovation opportunities from the group that are discussed and prioritised during the meeting. Topics typically range from exploring innovative ideas in macro-level areas, such as applications and data centres, all the way to specific disruptive trends such as cloud, mobile, social and big data.

The focus of the workshops can be business-, process- and technology-oriented, as opposed to just one particular slant, and we take the approach that all ideas don't necessarily have to be strategic or transformational in nature. Even tactical or incremental ideas, as long as they can lend measurable business value, are considered to be in scope and of benefit.

IN-DEPTH: INNOVATION WORKSHOP APPROACH

Innovation workshops are internal and customer-facing workshops that focus on innovation opportunity identification, categorisation, prioritisation and then the development of high-level business cases and implementation roadmaps for the most promising opportunities identified.

Key process steps

- **Opportunity identification** – Identify innovation opportunities for a specific business pain point or opportunity. Participants bring a laptop or tablet and enter their ideas into a web-based group decision support software (GDSS) tool, which provides electronic capture of ideas for discussion and voting.

- **Opportunity categorisation** – Discuss the identified opportunities by reviewing the electronic whiteboard of ideas and hearing the elevator pitches related to each idea. Categorise ideas by key focus area and remove duplicates.

- **Opportunity prioritisation** – Further classify the innovation opportunities by way of individual voting so that we gain a sense of their financial value, strategic fit, time/cost to implement/maintain, and project risk/complexity.

- **Opportunity profiling** – Complete high-level opportunity profiles for each innovation opportunity to better understand their business value (including more quantitative assessment of ROI impact and overall benefits) and suitable timing in terms of implementation.

- **Opportunity roadmapping** – Determine how these innovations can be more effectively built into a future state architecture and roadmap for subsequent implementation.

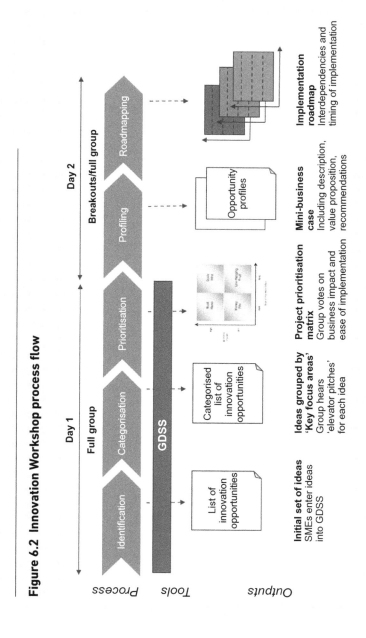

Figure 6.2 Innovation Workshop process flow

In conducting these sessions, here are ten best practices that I've found help to ensure quality outcomes when using this type of GDSS specifically for an Innovation Workshop:

1. **Agree on goals and objectives upfront with stakeholders** – Well ahead of the workshop, discuss the overall goals and objectives with your stakeholders and also prepare a list of key focus areas or topic areas for your workshop. These key focus areas help to define specifically what topics you wish to brainstorm around with your audience.

2. **Drive the selection of attendees based upon key focus areas** – The key focus areas should be used to determine the appropriate SMEs to invite to the session. Since the focus is a collaborative brainstorming session, as opposed to one-way presentations, it's useful to keep the total number of attendees to between 10 and 25.

3. **Present innovation challenges and opportunities to set the context** – Have your stakeholder present a short overview of the business needs related to innovation and the kinds of ideas he or she is looking for out of the session. This will help set the background context for the SMEs at the session.

4. **Prepare a well-defined agenda and participant guide** – The agenda should clearly mark out sections for opportunity identification (brainstorming), opportunity categorisation (hearing the elevator pitches for each idea and combining related ideas) and opportunity prioritisation (voting). For example, if you're using online software to capture ideas from the group, I've found that 30 minutes is an ideal amount of time for individuals to submit ideas into the system using their laptops and tablets.

5. **Allow participants to build upon each other's ideas** – Once attendees have entered their ideas into the software, it's useful to have them review the ideas from others and add comments as appropriate. This helps them to build upon each other's ideas and can help to strengthen the overall value proposition around the ideas or help to raise additional questions for consideration.

6. **Hear the elevator pitches for each idea** – Since ideas are submitted by everyone simultaneously, it's important to go down the electronic whiteboard of ideas row by row and hear the elevator pitches from the people who submitted them. This gives the full audience an overview of the ideas before moving to the voting stage.

7. **Use a well-defined set of voting criteria** – A well-defined set of criteria can help to ensure that voting results can be used to properly evaluate ideas based upon business benefit and ease of implementation. A best practice is to have an equal number of criteria for each of these two vectors so that innovation ideas and opportunities can be plotted on a cost/benefit matrix or similar analysis tool such as a project prioritisation matrix.

8. **Define how you will measure success** – To measure the success of the workshops, you'll typically want to track three key areas: the quality of the workshop session, the quality of the facilitators themselves and the business outcomes achieved as a result of the session. This can be achieved by attendee satisfaction surveys at the conclusion of the workshop and also by rigorous follow-up to monitor the success of ideas designated for further analysis and eventual implementation.

9. **Make the facilitation role strategic** – The facilitation role for innovation workshops is much more than just facilitating an audience: it entails managing the pre-workshop planning, the actual conduct of the workshop, and then the necessary follow-up actions to ensure that the desired business outcomes are realised as a result of the session.

10. **Maintain consistency and quality through frequent training** – If you put in place a programmatic approach to these kinds of innovation workshops, it's important to provide regular training for your facilitators and to select the right number of facilitators to cover your anticipated needs across business units and geographies. There's a delicate balance that needs to be maintained between having enough facilitators for coverage and a small enough group for quality purposes so that they can build their experience.

Of course, some of these guidelines will vary based on exactly how you define and implement your innovation workshops. What I've found over the years is that there's a number of ways to 'skin the cat' and no 'right' or 'wrong' approaches. Each approach has its own strengths and weaknesses and it's important to learn from each variation to the workshop approach and go with what fits best in your particular case. There's a tremendous number of variables you can adjust in an Innovation Workshop, from number of focus areas, to number of attendees, to the structure and timing of each step in the process, to the types of voting criteria and whether or not to vote individually or as a group. The key thing to bear in mind is that sometimes simplicity and consistency is the most effective approach.

KEEPING IT LEAN

As we have seen, innovation workshops are a valuable technique for event-based ideation, which can complement ongoing enterprise ideation processes. As with any enterprise initiative or capability with the word 'innovation' in its title, innovation workshops are also subject to the usual – and appropriate – scrutiny, evaluation and questions from various parts of the organisation, from senior leadership to managers and employees.

Commonly asked questions may revolve around the efficiency and effectiveness of the workshop in terms of any of the following aspects:

- methodology;
- duration;
- cost;
- resources;
- objectives;
- outcomes.

The questions are often inspired by the latest management approach such as 'lean', as well as (for obvious business purposes) to ensure and confirm a healthy ROI. Executives and employees may need reassurance that the workshop is not too 'heavyweight' in terms of being too process-heavy, too lengthy in duration, too costly in terms of employee time commitments and travel costs, or too inefficient in getting to its overall objectives and target outcomes.

As a digital business leader or manager, if you're coordinating any aspect of innovation for your organisation, particularly innovation workshops or other initiatives in support of targeted ideation, here are three steps to ensure that your activities pass – and even exceed – the litmus test in terms of 'lean' principles.

Lean processes

The first area to review is that of the process behind your Innovation Workshop. The process needs to be lightweight, flexible and tailorable to get to the required results quickly, but with the appropriate level of rigour, consistency and quality throughout.

The workshop process should go beyond just getting to a laundry list of ideas, and ideally should take these ideas from identification, to categorisation, to prioritisation (that is, voting) and finally, for the most promising ideas, to high-level business cases and an actionable roadmap. What happens 'after the workshop' should be equally agile and well defined.

It's important to look at the efficiency of every step of the workshop process from ideation to voting and optimise accordingly. For example, within the ideation process itself, we've found that we can collect electronically submitted ideas from a group in as little as 30 minutes, provided they have the right background context and guidance upfront to focus their efforts.

As another example, voting on ideas requires the right number of voting criteria that will provide sufficient data for interpretation and analysis, but without tying up too much time on the part of the participants. We've found that four voting criteria, with two as a measure of 'business impact' and two as a measure of 'ease of implementation', is a manageable number for voting purposes that can still provide sufficient insight for a project prioritisation matrix.

It's also useful to design and offer several versions of the workshop, ranging from a half-day to a one-day and two-day format, based on the number of process steps conducted and the size of your audience (see Table 6.1). We typically take ideation all the way through to voting via half-day and one-day sessions, based on audience size, and then progress to the development of high-level business cases and implementation roadmaps on the second day of our two-day sessions.

Table 6.1 Different types of Innovation Workshop based on scope and audience

Workshop type	'Lite'	'Standard'	'Standard'	'Extreme'
Process steps	3 steps (identification through prioritisation)	3 steps (identification through prioritisation)	3 steps (identification through prioritisation)	5 steps (identification through roadmapping)

(continued)

Table 6.1 (Continued)

Workshop type	'Lite'	'Standard'	'Standard'	'Extreme'
Location	Typically virtual	Physical, virtual or hybrid	Physical, virtual or hybrid	Typically physical
Typical audience	Internal	Internal or customer facing	Internal or customer facing	Customer facing
Typical number of attendees	10–15	15–20	15–25	10–25
Typical duration	~2 hours	~4 hours	4–6 hours	2 days
Typical number of ideas	40 with prioritisation	60 with prioritisation	80 with prioritisation	80 with prioritisation; 10–15 high-level business cases

The process should also support physical, virtual or hybrid sessions (that is, both physical and virtual attendees), based on the intended audience and the objectives of the workshop. As an example, you may wish to perform in-person workshops with clients where face time is paramount, but rely more on virtual or hybrid sessions for internal purposes.

Lean resources

In terms of resources, you want to ensure that you're bringing the right people to your session and have a robust programme in place in terms of how you train and deploy your Innovation Workshop facilitators.

For choosing the right attendees, a best practice is to use the key focus areas of the workshop as a way to drive the SME selection. This will ensure that you have the right people at the table – either physically or virtually – to cover the key topics for the session.

As an example, in running workshops for clients, I typically work with the client sponsor ahead of time to agree on the goals and objectives for the workshop, and to precisely define the key focus areas for the brainstorming. The key focus areas are typically six to eight major topic areas, where the client wishes to explore innovative ideas, and are used to determine the SME selection on both the client side and from my own organisation.

For facilitation, we draw from a global pool of trained facilitators. The goal is to have sufficient geographic and language coverage worldwide, but a small enough team so that the facilitators are running many sessions per year and can build their expertise. This helps to ensure quality and consistency in the workshops. You might think of it as a 'minimum viable footprint' approach in terms of enough facilitators for the global footprint, yet a small-enough, focused-enough team for quality and consistency.

Finally, if you have key physical locations where you know you'll be running multiple innovation workshops per year, having facilitators trained up locally can be another valuable approach to conserve travel costs.

Lean technology

In terms of lean technology, a cloud-based GDSS can be a powerful tool for capturing ideas, discussing and reviewing the ideas with the group (that is, hearing the elevator pitches), and then voting on the ideas based on business benefit and ease of implementation.

In comparing web-based workshops with traditional, manual workshop techniques, I've seen a twofold to fourfold increase in the number of ideas that can be generated and a far more efficient voting process.

In a typical Innovation Workshop, using a GDSS, we can capture 50 to 100 ideas from a group of 10 to 25 attendees and arrive at a prioritised set of the most promising ideas within two to six hours, based on audience size. In contrast, a 'traditional' innovation workshop using sticky notes, or similar, may generate half the number of ideas within the same time frame, and without any prioritisation of the ideas.

Table 6.2 shows some typical time requirements for the various steps in a fast-paced, two-day Innovation Workshop from idea capture, to elevator pitches, to voting, to development of mini-business cases and an overall implementation roadmap.

Table 6.2 Typical time requirements for a fast-paced, two-day Innovation Workshop

Process step	Typical time requirement	Comments
Day 1 (entire group)		
Opportunity identification (Capturing ideas within GDSS)	30 minutes	• Can generate 100 ideas within 30 minutes with 25 people (~4 ideas per person)
Opportunity categorisation (Hearing and discussing elevator pitches for each idea)	2–3 hours for 40–60 ideas	• Elevator pitches take around 2 hours for 40 opportunities (~3 minutes per opportunity)

(continued)

Table 6.2 (Continued)

Process step	Typical time requirement	Comments
Opportunity prioritisation (Voting on ideas within GDSS)	40–60 minutes for 40–60 ideas	• Voting takes about 1 minute per item (assuming elevator pitch discussions occurred earlier)
Day 2 (in breakout groups)		
Opportunity profiling (Developing mini-business cases)	2–3 hours for 4–6 opportunities	• Takes around 2 hours for 4 opportunities (~30 minutes per opportunity)
Opportunity roadmapping (Developing overall implementation roadmap)	2 hours for 30–40 opportunities	• Takes around two hours for 30–40 opportunities in total

Perhaps more importantly, the GDSS enables the entire set of participants to contribute ideas on an equal footing (that is, all have access to enter ideas electronically) as opposed to the manual, paper-based or whiteboard approach, which tends to favour the most vocal few in the room. This can be one of the unsung, yet important, value-added benefits of an Innovation Workshop, since it enables you to convene a cross-functional or cross-business unit team who may not collaborate on a regular basis. It enables cross-pollination of ideas and can help drive consensus.

While these are some specific recommendations related to innovation workshops, it's also important to apply the same thinking across your entire innovation management capability – of which we have seen there are typically five critical pillars.

Today's innovation programmes need to be highly adapted and fine-tuned to support digital transformation initiatives and should therefore embrace the same operating principles – that is, lean, agile, flexible, efficient and more – so they can be executed at speed and at scale.

KEY TAKEAWAYS FOR CHAPTER 6

- While ideation is a small part of an enterprise innovation programme, there's many things to consider in terms of targeting your ideation activities to support both the tactical and strategic needs of the business as it relates to digital transformation.

- In terms of ideation tools and approaches, there's no shortage of options to choose from. The key consideration is that you'll likely need a combination of both event-based ideation, as well as ongoing, enterprise-wide ideation processes as part of your overall innovation strategy.

- By implementing a multi-modal ideation approach, with both event-based and ongoing ideation vehicles, your organisation will be well poised to maximise the innovation potential across your diverse ecosystem of employees, customers, suppliers and partners in a systematic manner and equally able to mobilise ideation sessions as, where and when opportunities arise.

- Innovation workshops focus on innovation opportunity identification, categorisation, prioritisation and then the development of high-level business cases and implementation roadmaps for the most promising opportunities identified.

- There's a tremendous number of variables you can adjust in an Innovation Workshop: from number of focus areas, to number of attendees, to the structure and timing of each step in the process, to the types of voting criteria and whether or not to vote individually or as a group. The key thing to bear in mind is that sometimes simplicity and consistency are the most effective approaches.

- As a digital business leader or manager, if you're coordinating any aspect of innovation for your organisation, particularly innovation workshops or other initiatives in support of targeted ideation, there are three steps to ensure your activities pass – and even exceed – the litmus test in terms of 'lean' principles: lean processes, resources and technology.

7   TIMING YOUR MOVE BASED ON TECHNOLOGY MATURITY

You win battles by knowing the enemy's timing, and using a timing which the enemy does not expect.

Miyamoto Musashi[1]

With a knowledge of the technology adoption lifecycle, we can overlay our own model on top of this in terms of what kinds of business value we can expect to extract over time. As emerging technologies are adopted into the enterprise at various stages of their maturity by pioneers, early adopters, and the early and late majority, there are generally three windows of opportunity, or 'waves', where these technologies can be exploited. By understanding the nature and characteristics of each wave, and the wave that each technology trend is in at any point in time, leaders and organisations can best exploit their position for business model transformation (emerging wave), high competitive advantage (differentiating wave) or proven business value (business value wave).

TIMING YOUR MOVE INTO DISRUPTIVE TECHNOLOGIES

The IoT. Big data analytics. Intelligent automation. With so many disruptive technologies on the horizon, timing your move into each can make the difference between getting ahead of the competition and falling irreparably behind.

One thing that can help you gauge when to take up an emerging technology is the technology adoption life cycle.[2] This sociological model, invented by researchers at the University of Iowa who were studying the adoption of hybrid seed corn by farmers, illustrates that adoption typically follows a bell curve, with the first adopters being the innovators, followed by the early adopters, the early majority, the late majority and finally the laggards (Figure 7.1).

It can certainly be argued that, over the course of the 20th century, technologies were adopted at a faster and faster pace. For example, the telephone took 25 years to reach 10 per cent penetration[3] of US households, and another 39 years to reach 40 per cent. Midcentury, colour television took 18 years[4] (between 1954 and 1972) to reach 50 per cent adoption by US households. More recently, the smartphone needed just ten years to reach 40 per cent adoption by US consumers, and the tablet has reached 10 per cent penetration in less than three years.

Figure 7.1 The technology adoption lifecycle

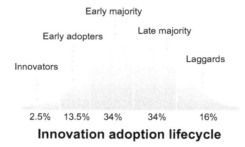

Source: Wikipedia.

Of course, a lot of factors come into play. Landline telephones and electricity took many years to be adopted by a majority of the population, but they both faced 'last mile' difficulties in bringing telephone lines and electric cables to homes. With colour television, price was a factor, as was the availability of colour programming. Nonetheless, as shown in Figure 7.2, the evidence points to ever-faster adoption rates, which can leave you thinking that there's a very short window for competitive advantage around each disruptive trend.

Figure 7.2 US technology adoption rates (1900–2014)

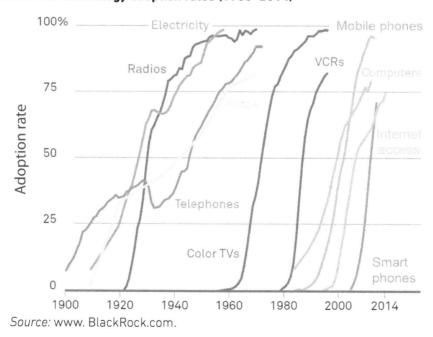

Source: www. BlackRock.com.

The good news is that, while product cycle times may be well under a year, the overall trend upon which the technologies are carried typically unfolds over many years. Within each trend there are multiple enabling technologies, all at various stages of maturity and adoption. Take cloud computing as an example. If we categorise cloud computing into software as-a-service (SaaS), platform as-a-service (PaaS) and infrastructure as-a-service (IaaS), it's clear that each area has its own unique trajectory and timeline. The SaaS movement has been under way since the late 1990s and is more mature than PaaS or IaaS. Even within the SaaS market, certain approaches and business functions are more mature and widely accepted than others. For example, cloud-based email and collaboration are far more widespread than current use of IT service management as-a-service.

In addition, many of the most enduring trends take many years to unfold. Mobility is a great example. While it's been around for several decades, it's only in recent years that we have the combination of low-cost, feature-rich devices, ubiquitous access, and easy-to-use applications and interfaces that has enabled mobility to quickly become the new desktop.

With all this in mind, timing your move into an emerging area is a lot more complex than a simple go/no-go decision. Whether it's the IoT, big data analytics or intelligent automation, here are three recommendations to help with timing your move:

1. Watch the early adopters

Even if they are in other industries, you can learn from the experiences of early adopters. If you're a fast follower as opposed to a lead innovator, you'll be able to study the experiences and case studies of companies and competitors in your industry in order to time your move. If you're a lead innovator, you may need to monitor other industries that may be faster adopters of emerging technology than your industry and see how their experiences might translate to opportunities within your own.

2. Determine a suite of strategic levers tailored to your corporate objectives

Develop a long list of ways you can apply the various technologies to benefit the business and detail what benefit will accrue to which set of stakeholders. It is likely that the levers can be applied toward either IT or line-of-business objectives and for any combination of cost reduction, process improvement, customer satisfaction or revenue generation purposes, depending upon the target business process and constituency. This suite of strategic levers will provide you with a slate of options that you can then apply over time, based upon the maturity of the underlying technologies and end-user readiness.

3. Develop a strategic roadmap for each disruptive trend

For each area like the IoT, big data analytics or intelligent automation, it's important to have a strategic roadmap over a suitable planning horizon, such as the next three years, which details how you plan to progressively exploit the technology for business advantage. These trend-specific strategic roadmaps should be a key part of your IT strategy, much the same way as the UK Government has taken a Digital by default[5] approach for all new digital services from the government, or the way in which the US federal government incorporated mobility into their Digital government strategy[6] and required agencies to mobile-enable at least two priority customer-facing services within a 12-month timeframe. The suite of strategic levers may give you a good starting point from which to map out your various initiatives within the roadmap.

Finally, it's important to know your company's overall stance and appetite for risk with regard to technology adoption and ensure that your plans are appropriately aligned. Even in a more conservative organisation, it may well be permissible and beneficial to break the mould if the stakes are not too high or if you're operating in a carefully controlled environment. In all situations, look for innovative uses of the technology above and beyond what others are doing. Many of the strongest business returns on emerging technologies often materialise when they're applied in novel ways to enable new business models and new business processes.

THE THREE WAVES OF DISRUPTIVE TECHNOLOGY ADOPTION

It's critical to maximising the business value of disruptive trends – such as the IoT, big data analytics and intelligent automation – that we understand their adoption lifecycles and leverage them appropriately at each stage. Having learned earlier in this chapter about the technology adoption lifecycle, we can now overlay our own model on top of this in terms of what kinds of business value we can expect to extract over time.

A particular technology trend in pioneer or early adopter status needs to be handled quite differently from when it's progressed into the early majority, or even the late majority. The kinds of benefits you can expect to obtain are quite different as well. Of course, we all know about the window of opportunity for competitive differentiation while the trend is in early stages of enterprise adoption, but let's explore this topic a bit further to see what other insights might be revealed.

An analogy I like to draw is surfing. I believe that there's three waves you can catch around the same technology trend: the emerging wave, the differentiating wave and the business value wave as shown in Table 7.1. That is, not only riding the wave around each disruptive trend, but riding the same wave of a particular trend multiple times during its journey to the shoreline. These three waves follow the adoption of the technology as it progresses from pioneers to mainstream adoption.

Table 7.1 The three waves of disruptive technology adoption

Wave	Emerging wave	Differentiating wave	Business value wave
Disruptive technology examples	• Blockchain technology • Intelligent automation • IoT • Wearable devices and AR	• Big data analytics • Social business	• Cloud computing • Mobile computing

(continued)

Table 7.1 (Continued)

Wave	Emerging wave	Differentiating wave	Business value wave
Technology adoption	Pioneers	Early adopters	Early and late majority
Business models	**NEW, POTENTIALLY TRANSFORMATIONAL** (e.g. Industrial Internet)	Unique, but formative business models	Well-defined business models and players
Competitive advantage/ differentiation	Differentiating, but within limited markets	**HIGH, DIFFERENTIATING** (e.g. data analytics for predictive maintenance)	Only moderate differentiation
Business value/ROI	Emerging examples of business value	Several commonly known ROI examples	**HIGH, WELL RECOGNISED** (e.g. SaaS cost reduction)

Understanding the wave that each trend is in at any point in time will help you to best exploit its position for business model transformation (emerging wave), high competitive advantage (differentiating wave) or proven business value (business value wave).

Let's look at each wave and examine some of its characteristics.

The emerging wave

The emerging wave relates to disruptive technologies and trends that are in the pioneer and early adopter stages. Trends such as the IoT, intelligent automation, wearable devices and AR, blockchain technology, SDNs and fabric computing are good examples for this wave since they're in the early stages of enterprise adoption. Because they're still emerging, there's tremendous potential for organisations to use them in unique ways to create new business models, deliver new digital products and services, and even explore and instill transformational changes within their industries.

At this stage, business models can be transformational, competitive advantage can be high in the specific areas of implementation, and the long-term ROI of an initiative or venture, if it's successful, can be outstanding. Outside the pioneers, however, the business value of the technology itself is often not clearly understood by the masses and there are limited examples of how it can be utilised for others to follow.

The differentiating wave

The differentiating wave relates to disruptive technologies and trends that are in the early adopter stages. Trends such as big data analytics and social business are currently in this wave, since they're still in relatively early adoption when you look at how the technologies are being utilised across the typical enterprise. There's still plenty of time for organisations to achieve competitive advantage and differentiation through these technologies by exploring untapped business scenarios and use cases that others have yet to either discover or exploit.

As an example, McKinsey's value levers for social business illustrate the many options available both within and across organisational functions.[7] Examples include leveraging social to 'forecast and monitor' operations and distribution functions, or leveraging social to 'co-create products' via open innovation with customers. While several social business value levers such as digital marketing and employee collaboration are in use by many, if not most, organisations there's still a number of value levers that are relatively untapped. In this wave, there are also several commonly known ROI examples for fast followers to pursue.

The business value wave

The business value wave relates to disruptive technologies and trends that are in the early and late majority stages. Trends such as cloud and mobile computing are clearly in this wave today, since the typical business models and scenarios for implementation are well defined, and the typical business value and ROI is well known and recognised. Examples include the use of SaaS for cost reduction and agility, or the use of mobile applications for sales force and field force productivity.

That's not to say that technologies in this wave can't be used for transformational business models or differentiation, but due to the maturity of the technology and its stage of adoption in the enterprise, this is typically less common or applies to new technical innovations within each megatrend. The technologies here are generally mature, well understood and are delivering value on a day-to-day basis. In essence, they've become part of the engine room for IT.

Key takeaways

So what are the key takeaways from this view on the disruptive trends? Think about how you could ride a wave around something like big data analytics or the IoT, not just for a new business model, such as carving out a role in an industry-specific data value chain (for example, device manufacturer, data provider, analytics provider, analytics integrator, etc.), but how you might ride other waves around this trend as it matures. How could you differentiate your products and services via insights from big data analytics, and how could you realise ongoing business value as it becomes part of business as usual?

One of the answers here lies in collaboration across the C-suite so that the business benefits of disruptive technologies are not only maximised across their lifecycle as they mature and evolve over time, but also across the enterprise in terms of putting IT to work as an enabler and amplifier of business performance.

KEY TAKEAWAYS FOR CHAPTER 7

- Timing your move into an emerging technology is a lot more complex than a simple go/no-go decision. Whether it's the IoT, big data analytics or intelligent automation, three recommendations to help with timing your move include watching the early adopters, determining a suite of strategic levers tailored to your corporate objectives and determining a strategic roadmap for each trend that can be incorporated into the overall technology roadmap.

- The suite of strategic levers across the organisation will provide you with a slate of options that you can then apply over time, based upon the maturity of the underlying technologies and end-user readiness.

- As emerging technologies are adopted into the enterprise at various stages of their maturity by pioneers, early adopters, and the early and late majority, we can overlay our own model to illuminate three windows of opportunity, or 'waves', where these technologies can be exploited.

- By understanding the nature and characteristics of each wave, and the wave that each technology trend is in at any point in time, leaders and organisations can best exploit their position for business model transformation (emerging wave), high competitive advantage (differentiating wave), or proven business value (business value wave).

- Collaboration across the C-suite is vital so that the business benefits of disruptive technologies are not only maximised across their lifecycle as they mature and evolve over time, but also across the enterprise in terms of putting IT to work as an enabler and amplifier of business performance.

PART III
ACTION – DIGITAL TRANSFORMATION STRATEGIES FOR SPECIFIC TARGET BUSINESS OUTCOMES

8 ENHANCING THE DIGITAL CUSTOMER EXPERIENCE

We see our customers as invited guests to a party, and we are the hosts. It's our job every day to make every important aspect of the customer experience a little bit better.

Jeff Bezos[1]

In Part I of this book, we saw how leading organisations are delivering compelling digital customer experiences via re-designed business models and processes, via combinations of foundational technologies, as well as by exploiting the power of platform and ecosystem-oriented business models. Each of these areas can be considered a strategic lever for creating or enhancing the digital customer experience by taking an outside-in approach to create compelling new customer journeys and value propositions.

In this chapter, we'll examine these strategic levers in more detail and take an in-depth look in terms of what the ideal digital customer experience may look like – in the form of a Digital Customer Experience (DCX) Bill of Rights. We'll also take a look at how combinations of foundational technologies can be used to provide a compelling next-generation experience in terms of 'digital experience essentials' and 'digital experience enhancers' at every step of the customer journey with your brand, product or service.

STRATEGIC LEVERS FOR THE DIGITAL CUSTOMER EXPERIENCE

Although it's not about the technology, as we've seen earlier, each foundational technology element can play a key part in contributing towards the overall, integrated experience from the customer's perspective looking from the outside in. While SMAC capabilities are now expected by default in leading consumer applications, the new competitive battleground is being fought with new weaponry that taps further into the power of personas and context, the IoT, wearables and AR, and intelligent automation. These capabilities can not only be applied to enhance and differentiate the digital customer experience, but they can also be used to help organisations better understand and manage their customers' digital journeys (Figure 8.1).

We'll now look at each of these strategic levers in more detail, beginning with the business model lever.

Figure 8.1 Strategic levers for the digital customer experience

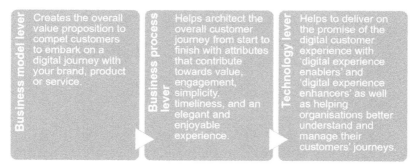

Business model lever

In Chapter 1, when we examined Porter's Five Forces Model of industry competition, we found that perhaps the strongest of the five forces is the bargaining power of buyers (that is, customers), since the biggest driver of digital business comes from the needs and expectations of consumers and customers themselves. This bargaining power lays out a new set of expectations for the digital customer experience and necessitates continual corporate and organisational innovation across business models, processes, operations, products and services.

Customers and consumers have amassed far more bargaining power today due to instant access to information, insights from social media (including access to reviews and feedback), low switching costs via digital channels, price sensitivity, access to sub-stitute products and services with greater ease of use and convenience, as well as increased industry competitiveness as a result of the other forces.

If you're operating at this level, you're likely constructing a completely new product or service for customers and crafting the digital customer experience and overall customer journey from the ground up. At this top level, you'll be addressing fundamental questions in regard to your business model and value proposition for customers as follows:

- **What's the scope, value proposition and differentiation of your overall solution?** This should include a description of the scope of the solution – that is, exactly what is being offered, the specific use cases for your target customers, and how the product or service fits into, or replaces, their current way of doing business. Clearly articulating the scope of the solution, including the starting and ending points in the customer journey, will help you to determine if you're attacking the right problem space, in terms of both market and customer appetite and your own ability to execute, or if you need to narrow your original vision to avoid trying to boil the ocean.

- **What's the detailed functionality of your product or service?** This should include a description of the key features and functionality, the enabling and disruptive technologies employed, and the overall technical architecture and deployment model, as well as the core intellectual property (IP) being employed and your envisioned product roadmap. In addition to your overall business model and partnering strategy, unique IP is key in terms of barriers to entry, since it may help to stave off the competition and other new entrants for at least a time sufficient for you to gain an edge.

- **What's the market you intend to serve, and what is its size and growth rate?** This should include answering the key question of why now is a good time for your specific solution, given the evolution of the market and recent market trends and developments – including changes to customer and buyer profiles, needs, expectations and behaviours. In addition, address what will compel customers to want to adopt and utilise your specific solution, instead of what's out there already, and what some of the envisioned drivers and barriers are to gaining this adoption.

- **Who is your target audience and what are your customer segments?** This should include a profile of your customers and buyers, their needs and, for business-to-business (B2B) scenarios, a list of initial prospects. If you have feedback from initial customer discussions, proofs of concept and pilots, this should be shared here as well to help validate customer demand and interest levels.

Answers to these questions, along with answers to other questions related to your business model, competition, partners, team and financials, can help to ensure that you've thought the plan through for your own purposes and that you will be best equipped to address stakeholder or investor scrutiny.

Doing your homework here will get you to a point where you can have an intelligent discussion, not only about the benefits of the platform or application you're envisioning, but also about the envisioned customer journey and how you believe you can realistically take the concept from idea to execution.

Business process lever

In Chapter 2, we learned that one of the key characteristics of a digital business process is that it's 'experience-centric', whereby the digital customer experience drives everything, powered by rich combinations of technology enablers. We learned that experience-centric digital processes, by their very nature, tap into powerful combinations of emerging and disruptive technologies as their foundational building blocks. We saw this earlier in our Streetline example, which taps into data from IoT sensors, relayed to the cloud, to publish real-time parking data via a mobile app so drivers can find open parking spots.

When we looked at the key attributes of a digital business process, compared to traditional business processes, we found that they were experience-centric, automated, simplified, digitised, personalised, dynamic, real time, granular, aggregated and scalable. Each of these attributes contributes in their own way towards the overall digital customer experience by helping to craft the overall customer journey from start to finish.

The net result is that, when applying this business process lever towards the digital customer experience, some of the resulting attributes translate to value, engagement, simplicity, timeliness, and an elegant and enjoyable experience. As an example, when processes are simplified down to their most intuitive, minimal steps, the outcome is a simple and timely digital customer experience. When processes have multiple versions and infinite configurations down to the individual customer, product or service, the result is that customers have a sense that they are well known and understood. When dynamic processes are created, deployed and executed on the fly, the net result is intelligent, anticipatory services. These are all examples of how business process re-design can be applied to craft compelling customer journeys that drive increased brand loyalty, customer satisfaction and revenues.

Technology lever

In Chapter 3, we saw how part of the secret to mastering digital business, and a key ingredient in some of the most successful business process re-design efforts using the 'digital medium', is utilising combinations of enabling technologies to create the most compelling digital customer experience possible. We saw how organisations can select powerful combinations of technologies to achieve target business outcomes ranging from enhancing the digital customer experience, to transforming the digital workplace, to optimising infrastructure and simplifying management.

When we think about applying the technology lever towards the digital customer experience, we can group these technologies into those that deliver 'digital experience essentials' and those that can be considered 'digital experience enhancers', which go above and beyond the essentials.

Digital experience essentials

In Chapter 4, we saw how social, mobile, analytic and cloud technologies, together with personas and context, and robust cyber security, were being used to improve the digital customer experience and create entirely new customer journeys. As an example, we saw how the Snapshot application from Progressive Insurance combines technology elements of a mobile device, extensive data analytics, a cloud-based application and 'badges' for good driving, which can be shared via the driver's social networks. We also saw how the driver's 'context' clearly comes into play, with the entire application focused on actual driving behaviour as monitored in real time by the Snapshot device.

We can think of these technologies as 'digital experience essentials' because they cater to basic customer needs and expectations such as the right to share, to be heard, and to be informed (social); the right to internet access anytime, anywhere (mobile); the right to information and recommendations (analytics); the right to simplicity and timeliness (cloud); the right to be known and understood (personas and context); and the right to safety and security (cyber security).

These are all critical elements where their presence, or absence, can make the difference between the services of digital leaders and digital laggards. Increasingly, having an in-depth knowledge and understanding about the customers' preferences, needs, interests and behaviours is becoming a defining characteristic of digital leaders. This information can be used to personalise the customer's digital journey at every stage along the way and to create a highly loyal customer base, where customers feel that they are intimately well known and their needs and expectations are well understood throughout every interaction and transaction. Examples of these highly personalised and curated experiences include Amazon's recommendation engine, Netflix's movie recommendations and many others.

Organisations that do this well have earned their customers trust by creating a win–win value proposition in terms of data sharing. Customers are willing to share their data, including their preferences, needs, interests and behaviours because they trust the company to use the information to deliver enhanced and highly personalised services and to respect their needs with regard to security and the privacy of their information. When we look across the digital experience essentials, data is one of the key elements because it's through data that organisations can really differentiate themselves by using this information to build a highly trusted relationship with their customers and one that is personalised and curated. As you apply the various strategy levers in crafting experiences for your own customers, data can be one of the most powerful weapons available.

Digital experience enhancers

As we look to the future, we are seeing a number of new technologies being applied as digital experience enhancers on top of the digital experience essentials. Examples include the IoT, intelligent automation technologies, as well as wearables and AR applications. These particular technologies are not necessarily required for a customer's digital experience, but certain companies are using them to carve out innovative spaces in their industries and to delight their customers with remarkable new experiences that are unlike anything that's come before. When we analyse these companies, we find that each company typically 'majors' in one of these digital experience enhancers and couples this with the full complement of digital experience essentials.

IoT enhancers

We saw an example of this in Chapter 4, with the Ring™ Video Doorbell.[2] Ring essentially 'majors' around the IoT by using IoT devices, including its wireless video doorbell, as the lead technology in its customer journey, together with a mobile app, video recording in the cloud and social features. As per our earlier Progressive Snapshot example, we see the familiar combination of SMAC technologies, but with the addition of IoT devices in this smart home scenario.

As another example, the Disney MagicBand is an IoT wristband that Disney visitors wear in order to enter the parks, unlock their Disney Resort hotel room and buy food and merchandise. According to Disney, each MagicBand contains an HF Radio Frequency device and a transmitter, which sends and receives RF signals through a small antenna inside the MagicBand and enables it to be detected at short-range touch points throughout Walt Disney World Resort.[3] It also connects to all the vacation choices and preferences they've made via their My Disney Experience website such as FastPass+ choices for selected attractions. While the RFID technology behind the MagicBand has been around for a while, what's interesting about this particular example is the way that Disney is using the wristband across a wide range of usage scenarios to enhance the overall customer experience.

Intelligent automation enhancers

If we look at some examples in the intelligent automation space, not only are companies delivering smart services by applying intelligent analytics and algorithms, including artificial intelligence (AI), to better understand and anticipate the customers' likely needs based upon their context and historical behaviour, but they're also pulling in robotics technologies directly into consumer environments.

The Aloft hotel chain in the US has been trialling robotic valets, from hospitality robotics company Savioke, since 2014. These robotic valets are used to autonomously deliver essentials to guests such as toothbrushes, snacks, extra towels and other supplies. This helps hotel staff focus more on serving guests around more important interactions, as opposed to mundane delivery tasks.[4] The robots can easily navigate the hotel passageways, including elevators, and deliver supplies directly from the front desk to the guest's room. The hotel staff simply put the supplies into a hatch at the top of the 3-foot-tall robot, type in the guest room number for the delivery and then send it off. The robot calls the elevator using a Wi-Fi connection and then calls the guest on their room phone when it arrives at the room. The overall customer experience is enhanced through both the novel interactions with the robotic valet, which can be a valuable and unique business differentiator, as well as through the enhanced attention of hotel staff.

As another example, the Henn-na hotel in the Huis Ten Bosch theme park in Nagasaki, Japan, has been aiming to become 'the most efficient hotel in the world' by reducing manpower and having 90 per cent of the staff be robotic. Robotic staff at this hotel include a robotic concierge, robotic porters for luggage, as well as small robotic creatures in the guest rooms that can switch on lights, provide weather forecasts and schedule wake-up calls.[5]

In these specific scenarios, both of these companies are experimenting with majoring in robotics via robotic staff and valets and then wrapping this experience with the complement of digital experience essentials. This innovation around intelligent automation isn't confined just to hotels, and robots are increasingly interacting with patients in hospitals, employees in the workplace, and in a wide range of physical and virtual scenarios. We'll explore this topic on intelligent automation in further detail in Chapter 9, 'Transforming the digital workplace', when we look at how it's impacting employees, augmenting work processes and reshaping the future of work.

Wearables and AR enhancers

Another set of digital experience enhancers are wearable devices such as smart glasses and smart watches coupled with AR applications. This enables users and applications to take advantage of the hands-free process optimisation and convenience of wearables, together with the instant information and intuitive visual guidance capabilities of AR applications.

Wearables and AR applications are extending the computing transformation that has defined the last several decades, in which computing has continually moved closer and closer to the specific point where work gets done. PCs moved computing from the data centre to the front office and then to users' desktops. The laptop, smartphone and tablet brought computing to our fingertips, wherever they might be. Wearables take this one step further by making computing devices even more lightweight, portable, unobtrusive and instantaneous. They open new modes of operation, from continual sensing and measurement, to navigating the physical environment, to facilitating instant information and collaboration.

The simple fact that wearable devices are hands-free gives them a distinct advantage over smartphones and tablets and, when coupled with AR applications, opens up a number of interesting application scenarios across consumer scenarios as diverse as retail, financial services, health care, transportation and government. Here are three use case scenarios by way of example:

- **Understanding and navigating the physical environment.** AR applications found early traction on smartphones. Already, we can use such apps to find restaurants, subway stations, hotels, ATMs, Wi-Fi hotspots and more, and we can even augment our driving and take measurements of physical objects. AR apps that help us to find things are increasing their utility when they are incorporated into wearable devices such as smart glasses and smart watches. As an example, even a few years ago, Google Glass provided a navigation app for drivers with a small display projected onto a corner of their glasses showing a live, interactive map with turning directions and time to destination. As another example, the American Airlines app on the Apple Watch includes features to help customers find Admirals Clubs, search for shops and restaurants, zoom and map their route with navigation to baggage claim or their connecting gate at several major airports with new interactive terminal maps.[6] As wearables move from the early adopter to the early mainstream in the next few years, businesses should think about how AR apps can help customers to find their stores, navigate their facilities, determine whether a product is in stock, check wait times, report product issues and more.

- **Enhancing the shopping experience.** In retail, AR technology has already made it possible for phones to act like barcode scanners and offer up extra product information, reviews and price comparisons. With wearable devices, AR apps can offer the same kinds of functionality but in a far more convenient manner, so consumers can continue to pick up and handle items while doing their online research hands-free. Retail-focused AR companies have already produced virtual dressing rooms for trying on clothing at home, and it's likely that wearable glasses will simplify that and bring it to the showroom as well.

- **Facilitating instant information and collaboration.** The main consumer scenario with wearables and AR applications is that users will benefit from instant content and collaboration. Wearable devices will make it easier to access news and weather, get updates on flight status, send and reply to messages, dictate email, get on-screen translation, take photos and video clips, and videoconference so they can see what their collaborators are looking at. As we've seen in recent years, the main objection has been that wearable glasses will promote stealth photographing and videotaping, although there has also been concern among government agencies, such as the UK Department of Transportation, that wearable glasses will be a distraction when driving.[7]

As you look across the various digital experience enhancers, it's worth thinking about how one or more of these technologies could enhance your customer's experience by simplifying tasks, reshaping traditional buying patterns, or by providing high-value information in real time, based on their context and location. Each of these technologies increases the art of the possible so you can continue to iterate and improve your customer's digital journey.

BRINGING IT ALL TOGETHER: THE DIGITAL CUSTOMER EXPERIENCE BILL OF RIGHTS

When we look across the strategic levers for enhancing the digital customer experience, we can see that some companies – Amazon, Apple, Disney and Netflix among them – are doing things right. A highly positive digital customer experience drives customer satisfaction, which in turn leads to increased revenues and ongoing customer loyalty for businesses. Consumers now expect and even demand the same kinds of digital experiences from any company they deal with, regardless of industry.

The unfortunate truth, however, is that many organisations are harming their customers' digital experience – and in some cases their safety – on a regular basis. Customers can find themselves with limited access to personal data, discover that their connected vehicle can be digitally sabotaged, or experience a wide range of service quality and consistency issues along their digital journeys.

What's needed is a DCX Bill of Rights, along the lines of the UK Consumer Rights Act 2015 and the US Consumer Bill of Rights, which spells out a set of essential rights and protections for consumers in terms of their dealings with product and service providers.

Here are ten attributes of a world-class digital customer experience that might form the basis for a DCX Bill of Rights.

For every digital interaction or transaction, the customer should be afforded the following basic rights:

1. **The right to value and engagement.** Customers should be provided a compelling value proposition to engage with an organisation, and be accompanied and guided on their entire journey with the brand, product or service.
2. **The right to simplicity and timeliness.** Every interaction or transaction should be quick, easy, efficient and actionable. The process should be as optimised as possible via the digital environment with minimal effort (that is, clicks, swipes, keystrokes) required to rapidly accomplish a desired task, or to obtain a timely resolution.
3. **The right to an elegant and enjoyable experience.** All user interfaces and application designs should be elegant in terms of visual appeal, and enjoyable to use, in order to deliver a truly compelling and memorable customer experience.
4. **The right to anytime, anywhere access.** The experience should be seamless and convenient by supporting any device, anytime, anywhere with a smooth transition between devices, apps and networks, between physical and digital channels, and between departments within your organisation.
5. **The right to be known and understood.** The experience should be highly personalised and contextualised by always understanding the customers' context including their preferences, needs, interests, behaviours, location, language and sentiment at any point in time to the level at which they wish to share that information with you.

6. **The right to intelligent, anticipatory services.** All services should be smart by applying intelligent analytics and algorithms, including AI, to understand and anticipate the customer's likely needs based upon their context and historical behaviour. Customers should be pro-actively notified if they need to take action or make a decision.

7. **The right to share, to be heard and to be informed.** Customers should be able to share appropriate elements of their experience with others via social media, should be listened to and responded to, and should be provided with access to information and advice from others who can help to inform their decisions about the product or service.

8. **The right to information, analytics and recommendations.** Historical and real-time data and information from the customer's digital journey should be readily available, instantly accessible and downloadable, yet disposable (where permissible), based on customer preference and needs. Customers should be allowed to interactively analyse their data and be provided with recommendations to help them make informed decisions.

9. **The right to safety and security.** All digital interactions, and operations of digitally connected devices including vehicles, should be safe and secure with privacy and security integrated into the full end-to-end process by design. Security should be an integral part of the process without adding unnecessary extra steps that detract from the customer experience.

10. **The right to education and consent.** Information should be made readily available for the customer to understand more about your company, its digital processes, products and services – including the security of their transactions and the privacy of their data – to help them make educated decisions and purchases. In accordance with other privacy-related bills, customers should be able to control what information is shared with marketers and how such data is utilised.

The DCX Bill of Rights is not intended to replace current consumer rights, but to build upon them with new, additional rights specifically for the customer experience in the digital age.

You can think of this as a hierarchy with a foundation of mandatory legal and regulatory protections, followed by consumer rights such as those in the UK Consumer Rights Act 2015 and the US Consumer Bill of Rights, and then the DCX Bill of Rights as an optional set of rights that organisations, both commercial and public sector, may wish to adhere to.

These rights do more than spell out basic protections in terms of security and privacy; they can also help to serve as a checklist for how to create world-class digital experiences for your customers. As you craft innovative new digital experiences for your own customers, you can use the rights as a checklist to ensure your services are delivering the end game in terms of taking the outside-in perspective that today's digital consumers demand. You can also see how the strategic levers such as the business process lever and the technology lever can be applied to help support and deliver one or more of these rights (Table 8.1).

Table 8.1 The DCX Bill of Rights enabled via business process levers and technology levers

DCX Bill of Rights	Business process lever	Technology lever
1. The right to value and engagement.	The digital customer experience drives everything, powered by rich combinations of technology enablers.	Platforms can enhance engagement by consummating matches and creating network effects that improve participant value as the platform grows.
2. The right to simplicity and timeliness.	Processes are simplified down to their most intuitive, minimal steps.	Cloud technology can enable customers to access services on demand in a flexible, pay-as-you-go model.
3. The right to an elegant and enjoyable experience.	Processes are highly automated and incorporate seamless hand-offs between humans and machines.	Elegant user interface and application design coupled with intelligent automation, social and gamification elements can provide elegant, streamlined and enjoyable experiences.
4. The right to anytime, anywhere access.	Physical distances become irrelevant and are often completely removed from the equation.	Mobility can enable customer access anytime, anywhere with re-designed business processes for faster, improved experience.
5. The right to be known and understood.	Processes have multiple versions and infinite configurations down to the individual customer, product or service.	Personas and context can help to understand the customer preferences, needs, interests, behaviours, location, language and sentiment at any point in time.
6. The right to intelligent, anticipatory services.	Dynamic processes are created, deployed and executed on the fly.	Intelligent analytics and algorithms, including AI, help to understand and anticipate customer needs based upon their context and historical behaviour.
7. The right to share, to be heard and to be informed.	Fine-grained measurements enable more precise process design.	Social computing can enable customers to share, be heard and be informed via social channels.
8. The right to information, analytics and recommendations.	Real-time data informs and optimises processes.	Big data analytics can enable customers to interactively analyse their data and be provided with recommendations to help them make informed decisions.

(continued)

Table 8.1 (Continued)

DCX Bill of Rights	Business process lever	Technology lever
9. The right to safety and security.	Processes are made secure by design based on relevant security policies and regulations.	Cyber security can enable customer safety with privacy and security integrated into the full end-to-end process by design.
10. The right to education and consent.	Processes enable users to control what information is shared with other entities and how such data is utilised.	Big data analytics can enable a 360-degree view of the customer to better serve their needs and support regulatory compliance.

Of course, the first step in mastering the digital customer experience is to master the physical customer experience. A great digital customer experience can be sabotaged if the physical customer experience is less than optimal. With all these elements in place, your organisation will be well positioned in placing the customer first, delivering a mutually rewarding experience, and competing in the age of digital disruption.

KEY TAKEAWAYS FOR CHAPTER 8

- The three strategic levers for enhancing the digital customer experience are the business model lever, the business process lever and the technology lever.

- 'Digital experience essentials' cater to basic customer needs and expectations such as the right to share, to be heard and to be informed (social), the right to internet access anytime, anywhere (mobile), the right to information and recommendations (analytics), the right to simplicity and timeliness (cloud), the right to be known and understood (personas and context), and the right to safety and security (cyber security).

- 'Digital experience enhancers' such as the IoT, intelligent automation technologies, wearables and AR applications are being used by certain companies to carve out innovative spaces in their industries and to delight their customers with remarkable new experiences that are unlike anything that's come before.

- The DCX Bill of Rights can help to serve as a checklist for how to create world-class digital experiences for your customers. As you craft innovative new digital experiences for your own customers, you can use the rights as a checklist to ensure your services are delivering the end game in terms of taking the outside-in perspective that today's digital consumers demand.

9 TRANSFORMING THE DIGITAL WORKPLACE

> I see robotic technology getting rid of the dangerous, the dirty, and the just plain boring jobs. Some people say, 'You can't, People won't have anything to do.' But we found things that were a lot easier than backbreaking labor in the sun and the fields. Let people rise to better things.
>
> Rodney Brooks[1]

Just as we saw in the previous chapter on enhancing the digital customer experience, where we looked at digital experience essentials and digital experience enhancers, there are a number of foundational and disruptive technologies transforming the future workplace for employees. Key among these are mobility, wearables, AR, social networks, intelligent automation, sensors and robotics. In this chapter we'll explore how 'instrumenting the human' with wearables and sensors and 'socialising the machine' with more natural, human-friendly capabilities is helping to optimise the blend of human–machine participation and interaction within the digital workplace.

INSTRUMENTING THE HUMAN AND SOCIALISING THE MACHINE

When it comes to the digital workplace, the popular opinion, and fear, is that machines are encroaching upon human work activities and taking an ever larger percentage of this work away for good – from the dirty and dangerous, to the dull, to decisions. Fortunately, this doesn't take into account the realm of possibilities created when work processes are re-imagined in the context of mutual human–machine collaboration.

By instrumenting the human and socialising the machine, we can re-design business processes to optimise the blend of human–machine participation and interaction – and complete tasks far more efficiently than either could individually. Industrial robots, such as those seen in a variety of manufacturing settings, have been around for a long time but have typically been kept separate from humans and even behind cages, in some cases for safety reasons. Today, machines are stepping out from behind the cage, and humans are stepping into their worlds.

Passing the baton between human and machine

As Julia Kirby and Thomas H. Davenport pointed out in their article 'Beyond automation' for *Harvard Business Review*,[2] rather than a zero-sum game, robotic automation can be thought of as augmentation, where humans and machines collaborate to get work done. This is akin to a relay where the baton is passed between human and machine working toward a common goal, as opposed to a race pitting one against the other.

Clearly, for business managers, in addition to reaping the benefits of this collaboration, it's also important to have a clean hand-off of the baton every time to optimise the process even further.

Since humans are driving the innovation around automation and robotics, we're consciously (and perhaps unconsciously) carving out our future roles in the workplace side by side with machines. Rather than harsh boundaries between humans and machines, we're creating a converged future where work processes are being optimised in two converging directions: instrumentation of human processes and socialisation of machine processes, so the two can work in greater harmony together.

Mapping the division of labour: human–machine collaboration

If we analyse this collaboration, we can see several distinct classes of work activity where either machines augment human processes, humans augment machine processes, or both (see Figure 9.1).

To illustrate the types of collaboration that can occur, it's useful to think of who performs the work in terms of human or machine, and whether the work is delivered physically or virtually. The set of human–machine scenarios includes the following:

- **'Physical–physical'** – meaning both humans and machines play a physical role such as caregivers working with smart mobile robots to deliver medicines and supplies in hospitals.

- **'Physical–virtual'** – meaning humans play a physical role and machines play a virtual role at the point where work is performed, such as warehouse employees using smart glasses for navigation and picking instructions to boost productivity.

- **'Virtual–physical'** – meaning humans play a virtual role at the point work is performed and machines play a physical role such as doctors performing telepresence surgery.

- **'Virtual–virtual'** – meaning both humans and machines play a virtual role such as in call centres, with human agents working in tandem with virtual cognitive agents.

Interestingly, whether humanoid or non-humanoid, and whether working physically or virtually, the various robots concerned are all being socialised to perform their unique tasks most effectively. Physical robots are being socialised to operate seamlessly within human spaces and adhere to human behavioural norms, and virtual robots are being socialised via their appearance and natural language capabilities.

The key point is that it's not just machines that are getting social; it's that humans are getting instrumented as well, all of which amplifies the possibilities to optimise work activities. Let's look at some examples of both of these areas.

Figure 9.1 Human–machine work scenarios where machines augment humans and vice versa

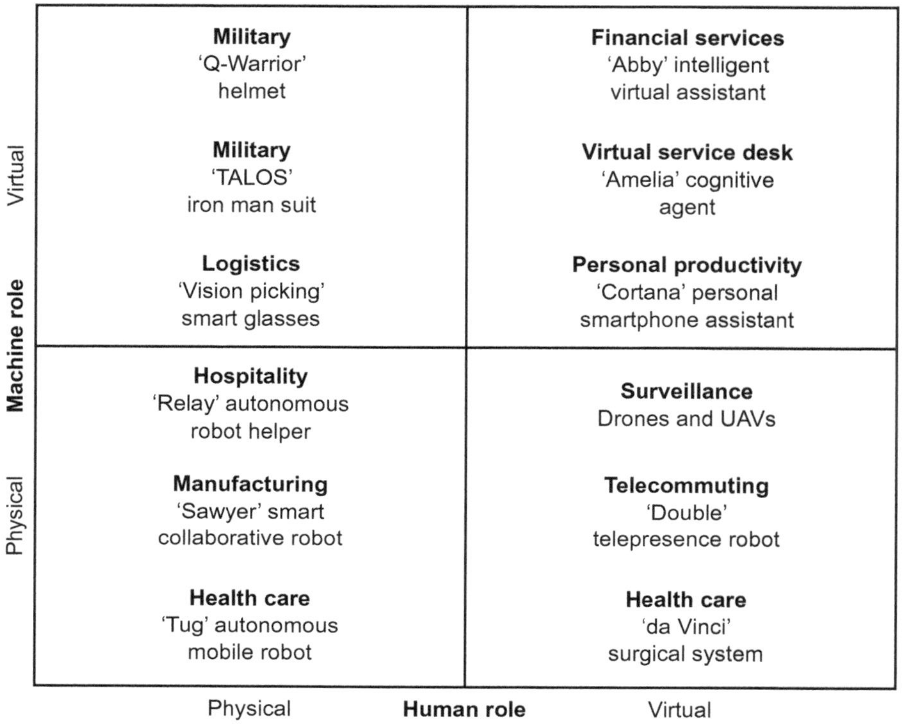

	Military 'Q-Warrior' helmet	**Financial services** 'Abby' intelligent virtual assistant
Virtual	**Military** 'TALOS' iron man suit	**Virtual service desk** 'Amelia' cognitive agent
	Logistics 'Vision picking' smart glasses	**Personal productivity** 'Cortana' personal smartphone assistant
	Hospitality 'Relay' autonomous robot helper	**Surveillance** Drones and UAVs
Physical	**Manufacturing** 'Sawyer' smart collaborative robot	**Telecommuting** 'Double' telepresence robot
	Health care 'Tug' autonomous mobile robot	**Health care** 'da Vinci' surgical system
	Physical	Virtual

Machine role / Human role

Instrumenting the human

As consumers, we're all becoming instrumented and taking advantage of the wealth of wearables and sensors now on the market. This 'quantified self' concept helps us to monitor our health and fitness and take advantage of the masses of data that are produced as we go about our daily lives. The pace of instrumentation is picking up in the workplace as well, as employers seek to track employee behaviour and optimise work activities.

Steve Cousins, CEO of Savioke, a company that manufactures autonomous robot helpers for the services industry, sees smart watches, as well as smartphones, as a powerful way for his team to connect into their robots currently deployed in trials at the Aloft hotel chain. This modern-day 'telepathy', as Steve sees it, helps employees to monitor the robots at scale and intervene in rare cases of exceptions where the robots need a helping hand.

In the logistics arena, DHL found that by instrumenting its warehouse pickers with smart glasses, together with AR software, it was able to improve the picking process by 25 per cent. By instrumenting its workers in this manner, compared to handheld devices,

DHL was able to move to a 'hands-free' optimised process where workers claimed they barely felt the glasses once they were wearing them.

At the higher end of the spectrum, in terms of wearables, initiatives such as the Q-Warrior helmet and the TALOS 'Iron Man' suit in the military are instrumenting soldiers to radically improve their situational awareness, giving them super-human capabilities.

In virtual work scenarios, the 'Double' telepresence robot, 'da Vinci' surgical system, and manually piloted drones and unmanned aerial vehicles (UAVs) are all examples of how we're instrumenting humans to be able to extend our reach and conduct work in remote locations.

Socialising the machine

In health care, Aethon's Tug robot is a smart autonomous robot that delivers medicines and supplies in hospitals. Having logged over 1 million miles in hospitals to date, it has been socialised to safely navigate around people and obstacles and can even take the elevator. One of the aspects of its socialisation is that it makes use of existing hospital facilities and infrastructure and doesn't need dedicated hallways or large docking areas.

Jim Lawton is Chief Product and Marketing Officer at Rethink Robotics. The company makes the Baxter industrial robot, well recognised by its iconic 'face screen'. One of the many ways Rethink Robotics has socialised its robots is by implementing anticipatory intelligence so the robot physically communicates where it's about to move. It does this by moving its head, its eyes, and then its arm when reaching for objects to instill a comfort level with workers who are shoulder to shoulder with the machine.

Rethink is bringing instrumented workers into the equation as well. Its new Sawyer robot has a second screen capability where supervisors can use a tablet to gain access to robot performance across the fleet. In addition, Lawton and the team are exploring how operational data gathered from 'smart robots and smart workers' can be analysed to further optimise work cells in manufacturing.

IPSoft's Amelia is a cognitive virtual employee that speaks, reads, writes and learns on the job, just like a human employee. According to Jonathan Crane, the company's chief commercial officer, she has emotions and intelligence, so she understands what people ask, even what they feel, and can empathise in both her facial and spoken response. If Amelia doesn't understand a request, she transfers the caller to an agent, then observes and learns so she can do it herself the next time. Amelia is being used in call centres to transform the labour mix with 'virtual engineers'. This helps 'automate the tactical, and populate the strategic', according to Jonathan, letting staff focus on higher-value-added projects and typically reducing labour costs by 30 to 35 per cent.

Even when we look at fully autonomous vehicles such as self-driving cars, the cars are being socialised to be overly cautious when manoeuvring to help avoid surprises for passengers and pedestrians alike. Soft robotics is another area of innovation where robots are being designed with soft and deformable structures to work with unknown objects, in rough terrains, or with direct human contact.

Implications for managers

So, given these two converging themes of instrumenting the human and socialising the machine, what are the implications for managers?

Over time, we'll start to see more scenarios toward the centre – more highly instrumented humans and more highly socialised machines working together. The business enablers won't be just one technology. The instrumented human will combine sensors, wearables and AR with powerful analytics delivered via the cloud, while the socialised machine will combine sensors, geolocation, expressive behaviours, empathy, knowledge, memory and speech.

We can also expect human–machine collaboration to operate at scale. We'll see one-to-one interactions, as well as one-to-many and many-to-many interactions as benefits are scaled up across the enterprise. Google's recent patent envisioning cloud control of an army of robots is just one example.

The specific human–machine scenarios will change over the duration of a particular customer's journey or a worker's business process. For example, within an airport setting, instrumented passengers will use a smart watch for notifications and way-finding, and will interact with an array of robots including self-service bag drop machines, robotic butlers to handle luggage and even robotic valets to park their cars.

Adriaan den Heijer, Senior Vice President at Air France-KLM, sees numerous applications where robotics can play a role from the passenger side, where we can find answers by combining robotics together with the human touch, to baggage handling robots that free up employees to become process operators.

The key for managers in the years ahead will be flexibility and finding the sweet spot for human–machine collaboration based on the nature of the work. Anywhere on the continuum is fine in terms of human instrumentation and machine socialisation, and the precise location is task dependent.

Workers will need to be adaptable for these different scenarios with machines, just as adaptability is paramount when working with other humans. Machines will need to be highly adaptable as well, as evidenced by the recent winner of the Defense Advanced Research Projects Agency (DARPA) robotics challenge, which was able to roll on four wheels as well as walk on two legs.[3] For managers envisioning the future digital workplace, consider the full range of options available – instrument and socialise whenever possible to create smooth, optimised interfaces where you can hand-off the baton in record time.

CASE STUDY: AMAZON

Transforming delivery services

In July 2016, online retailer Amazon teamed up with the UK Government to 'explore the steps needed to make the delivery of parcels by small drones a reality'.[4] One of Amazon's goals is to use drones to safely deliver parcels to customers within 30 minutes of the time the order is placed online. In addition to having an anticipated positive impact on the digital customer experience in terms of improved delivery times and an altogether different way of receiving your parcels, this initiative and others like it represent some significant changes for the digital workplace as well.

In this scenario, rather than driving traditional delivery vans, workers will be piloting fleets of drones. This is yet another example of human–machine collaboration in the future digital workplace where the work is performed in a virtual–physical scenario with remote human pilots controlling tens or even hundreds of drones performing at-home delivery.

Operating from Amazon distribution centres, under the brand of Amazon Prime Air, the drones are able to fly for several miles at speeds of around 50 mph carrying loads weighing up to 5 lb. Some of the key operating parameters for the Amazon drones are listed in Table 9.1. Current US Government restrictions limit drones to line-of-sight operation, with each drone having a physical pilot controlling it from the ground. Clearly for this kind of business model to succeed financially, the drones need to be piloted beyond line of sight, with workers operating far more than one drone at a time.

Table 9.1 Fast facts about the Amazon drone technology

Drone operating attribute	Operating parameter
Airspace	200–400 feet
Operating range	Several miles
Speed	50 mph
Delivery time	Under 30 minutes
Cargo capacity	5 lb
Anti-collision technology	Sensors and vehicle-to-vehicle (V2V) communications
Power supply	Batteries
Location technology	GPS and on-board cameras

The Amazon initiative, in the concept stage at the time of writing, aims to explore some of these challenges and opportunities by looking at:

> beyond line of sight operations in rural and suburban areas, testing sensor performance to make sure the drones can identify and avoid obstacles, and flights where one person operates multiple highly-automated drones.[5]

Other companies such as Matternet, based in Menlo Park, California, are taking a slightly different approach to piloting their drones by using autonomous drones that operate between pre-defined routes, using a mobile application to select the destination and to initiate take-off. Matternet's drones are being used in production in many Third World countries and elsewhere to deliver medical supplies in hard-to-reach areas.

Whether human-piloted or completely autonomous, drone technology is revolutionising last mile logistics and is continuing to push the envelope in terms of how digital business is performed from city centres to some of the most remote places on earth.

KEY TAKEAWAYS FOR CHAPTER 9

- Since humans are driving the innovation around automation and robotics, we're consciously (and perhaps unconsciously) carving out our future roles in the workplace side by side with machines.

- Rather than harsh boundaries between humans and machines, we're creating a converged future where work processes are being optimised in two converging directions: instrumentation of human processes and socialisation of machine processes, so the two can work in greater harmony together.

- By instrumenting the human and socialising the machine, we can re-design business processes to optimise the blend of human–machine participation and interaction – and complete tasks far more efficiently than either could individually.

- Whether humanoid or non-humanoid, and whether working physically or virtually, the various robots concerned are all being socialised to perform their unique tasks most effectively. Physical robots are being socialised to operate seamlessly within human spaces and adhere to human behavioural norms, and virtual robots are being socialised via their appearance and natural language capabilities.

- The key for managers in the years ahead will be flexibility and finding the sweet spot for human–machine collaboration based on the nature of the work. Anywhere on the continuum is fine in terms of human instrumentation and machine socialisation, and the precise location is task dependent.

10   GAINING INSIGHTS FROM ANALYTICS

Information is the oil of the 21st century, and analytics is the combustion engine.

Peter Sondergaard, Gartner Research[1]

Throughout our examination of mastering digital business, we've seen examples of how information and data are playing a fundamental yet highly differentiating role across all aspects of digital transformation. New sources of data and new ways of storing, processing and analysing this data are being used to enable new platform business models, to create new value-added services by tapping into the data swirling around existing products and services, to differentiate the digital customer experience, to improve operational efficiencies (as we saw in our Industrial Internet scenarios such as manufacturing), to enable breakthrough performance (as we saw with the Mercedes AMG Petronas Formula One Team) and much more.

According to Tom Reilly, CEO of Cloudera, a data analytics company, the last six to ten years have seen the world become highly inter-connected. We're now connected to a tremendous amount of data coming in from smartphones, apps, social media, and an increasing number of sensors and IoT devices. This newly connected world is creating both threats and opportunities for every industry and every company. According to IDC,[2]

By 2020, organizations able to analyze all relevant data and deliver actionable information will achieve an extra $430 billion in productivity benefits over their less analytically oriented peers.

Correspondingly, the use cases for leveraging this information via big data analytics are now a board-level discussion.

In this chapter, we'll pull all this together to explore and summarise the key board-level use cases for big data analytics, the strategies for how to think about exploiting this data in unique new ways, and the architectural approaches to transform your existing data infrastructure to enable a truly data-driven enterprise.

BOARD-LEVEL USE CASES FOR BIG DATA ANALYTICS

In the world of big data, we've heard for many years about the 3Vs – namely, the volume, velocity and variety – of big data that differentiate it from the traditional highly structured data we're used to working with in the years, and even decades, past.

In terms of volume, the digital universe is doubling in size every two years and will reach 44 trillion gigabytes by 2020, up from 4.4 trillion gigabytes in 2013.[3] It's estimated that most companies in the US have at least 100 terabytes of data stored.[4] It's also estimated that organisations typically only analyse about 5 per cent of this data, so clearly new techniques are required to store and analyse this ever-increasing volume of information.

In terms of velocity, real-time data is now streaming in from an ever-increasing number of sensors and IoT devices as well as from countless customer interactions and transactions worldwide. As we saw earlier, the Mercedes AMG Petronas Formula One Team now collects more data within a single race weekend than they did across every race weekend from 1998 to 2006 combined. Given approximately 16 to 19 races per Formula One racing season, this equates to over 150 times the data volume being collected compared to prior years. The New York Stock Exchange captures 1 terabyte[5] of trade information during each trading session. On the consumer side, if we look at the fourth annual installment of the 'Data Never Sleeps' study by business intelligence and data visualisation company, Domo,[6] we find that every single minute of every day, there are:

- 69,500,000 words translated by Google;
- 18,264,840 MB of data consumed by US wireless users;
- 3,567,850 text messages sent in the US;
- 99,206 requests answered by Siri;
- 86,805 hours of video streamed by Netflix subscribers.

New techniques to deal with the velocity of big data need to clearly support the processing and analysis of real-time streaming data – from people, things and organisations – so that business decisions can be made as soon as information is captured and insights are revealed.

In terms of variety, data is now coming in from a wide array of sources ranging from social media, to IoT devices, to live video feeds and much more. It's estimated that 70 to 80 per cent of an organisation's data is now unstructured, so this presents a large opportunity for analysis and decision making. New techniques to deal with the variety of big data need to make both structured and unstructured information readily and equally available, so that insights can be generated by looking across all data sources.

In its early years, big data discussions were confined to the 'what' of big data in terms of describing the 3Vs and even adding a fourth V of 'veracity'. Organisations were focused on tools and technology and experimented with various big data pilots and proof of concepts to test out the technology and uncover the technical possibilities. Today, organisations are moving on to the 'why', 'how' and 'where' of big data in terms of why it's of business benefit, and how and where it can be applied in production deployments across the business.

So what are the key board-level use cases now that the concept of big data has been around for several years and organisations have moved well beyond discussions about tools and technology and are now squarely focused on exploiting the most promising use cases they can uncover? While there are hundreds of use cases for gaining insights from analytics, if we distil them down in terms of a factor analysis, we find that they can be grouped into three key areas:

- customer insights;
- operational insights;
- risk management insights.

These three types of insights, and their corresponding sources of data and typical benefits are illustrated in Table 10.1. In all three of these use cases, organisations can additionally use the insights from big data analytics to create new digital services and even entirely new business models.

It's important to mention that there's also some overlap and connectivity between these use cases, especially when it comes to the sources of data for each of them. For example, customer insights can be informed not only from data from customers, but also from data from things. This is the data that can be captured about the customer's usage of your products, whether it's a car, a home appliance, a fitness band or even a toothbrush. This is what I call the 'Internet of Behaviours'. It's the detailed usage and behavioural data that's collected as individuals use various IoT devices and systems. It provides compelling insights that organisations can use to gain a better understanding of their customers in terms of their preferences, behaviours and interests.

Table 10.1 Key board-level use cases for big data analytics

Types of insights	Sources of data	Typical benefits
Customer insights	Data from customers – explicit and implicit data from preferences, needs, interests, behaviours, usage, interactions and transactions.	• Improved customer satisfaction from more personalised services • Increased revenue from new data-driven services • Reduced customer churn
Operational insights	Data from things – sensors, devices, computers, machines, fleets and factories.	• Improved operational efficiencies • Cost savings from predictive maintenance • Cost savings from improved operations
Risk management insights	Data from customers or things representing anomalous patterns of behaviour.	• Reduced business risk • Improved compliance • Improved cyber security

Customer insights

We saw earlier in Chapter 8, 'Enhancing the digital customer experience', how analytics is one of the key 'digital experience enablers' contributing to the overall digital customer experience. Not only does it appear explicitly in two of our ten DCX Bill of Rights (that is, 'The right to be known and understood' and 'The right to information, analytics and recommendations'), but it can also be argued that it underpins every single 'right'. Data is perhaps the single most important digital experience enabler because it can provide true insights to help organisations understand customer preferences, needs, interests, behaviours, location, language and sentiment at any point in time.

According to Mr Reilly, with more information available now than ever before, we can use this data to predict and anticipate customer needs and translate this into business outcomes that are significant for board members. As an example, in the telecommunications industry, organisations can use their customer insights to reduce customer churn by anticipating, predicting and reaching out to customers who are showing signs of unhappiness. This can be detected in the data by analysing dropped customer support calls, social media postings and so on. Improving customer churn even by one or two percentage points can be worth hundreds of millions of dollars, which would otherwise be lost to the competition.

In the banking industry, understanding customers across all physical and digital channels (for example, branch, web, mobile, voice, email and chat) can help to build a 360-degree profile of the customer. This profile can be used to better understand the customer's household and anticipate their financial needs. For example, you may know that your customer is about to take a vacation and may be able to offer them a suitable loan to help cover their expenses.

In the health care industry, monitoring and understanding a patient's health status and activity, including diet and exercise, between their scheduled doctor or hospital visits, and pro-actively reaching out to them with advice and support, can help to reduce the number of visits required and thus translate into more effective and cost-efficient delivery of health care.

Operational insights

We saw earlier in Chapter 4 how analytics is being used as a key service within platform business models such as the GE Predix platform to support use cases such as predictive maintenance. By collecting and analysing the data from industrial assets, organisations can gain real-time insights that can help to optimise industrial infrastructure and operations at the individual asset level or even across their entire fleet or set of factories.

These operational insights can be applied to improve IT performance as well as business performance. Data analytics company, Cloudera, for example, instruments its software so it essentially 'phones home' to provide a health check. This enables Cloudera to pro-actively predict which customers in their environments are about to have a problem. In fact, 20 per cent of Cloudera customer support cases are now created by Cloudera on the customer's behalf. Mr Reilly anticipates that soon organisations across many industries will be shifting their paradigm from retroactively fixing assets and infrastructure to pro-actively maintaining their assets and infrastructure before they experience issues.

As an example of the business benefits of gaining operational insights, Siemens PLM, a software company in the enterprise manufacturing and supply chain space, was able to realise an annual saving among its client base conservatively estimated at between $15 and 25 million, based on its client's ability to identify and address supply chain issues in near real time. Siemens utilised an enterprise data hub (EDH) within their supply chain product quality solution, Omneo™, to gain a 360-degree view of product performance across the supply chain – from suppliers, manufacturing, equipment, field service and repair/re-manufacturing operations. The increased visibility enabled by this solution via the use of big data analytics meant that problems could be identified and addressed as soon as they started occurring, enabling Siemens' manufacturing clients to spend more time resolving challenges and less time trying to locate them.[7]

Reduced business risk

When it comes to reducing business risk, some of the key data analytics use cases in this category include security analytics, anti-money laundering and fraud detection. Since today's cybercriminals are so advanced with their tools and techniques, organisations can't rely on signature-based detection methods anymore and need to look at user behaviour and anomaly detection instead. This anomalous behaviour can come from cybercriminals or even from employees in terms of an insider threat. Apache Hadoop (the foundation of Google's IT infrastructure), with its ability to process large quantities of real-time data, is becoming a pre-eminent tool for conducting security analytics to detect these kinds of issues.

The same techniques can also be applied when looking for fraudulent activities or when looking to prevent money laundering. If an organisation detects anomalous behaviour, then it can examine that behaviour in more detail with sophisticated pattern matching algorithms looking across various digital breadcrumbs to determine if there is underlying fraud or money laundering underway.

As an example of reduced business risk, Markerstudy, a leading UK-based general insurer serving over 1.75 million customers, was able to reduce claim fraud with savings of £5 million and increase their new policy count by 120 per cent in 18 months. The insurer used a big data analytics platform powered by Apache Hadoop across key areas of its operation, including customer insights, risk and underwriting, as well as real-time fraud detection and prevention.

CASE STUDY: MARKERSTUDY

REAL-TIME CLAIMS FRAUD DETECTION AND PREVENTION

Background
Markerstudy is a leading UK-based general insurer serving over 1.75 million customers. The company was established in 2001 and provides insurance solutions primarily

through a network of over 3,000 brokers and intermediaries. With annual revenues of over £1.4 billion, the company specialises in commercial and personal auto including niche sectors such as young drivers, high performance cars, taxis and fleet insurance.

Challenge

One of the primary business drivers for Markerstudy to move to a big data analytics platform was to enhance the performance of its common portal for centralised rating for intermediaries. The portal, called the Insurer-Hosted-Rating Hub, was seeing increasing volumes of data and generating close to 25 million quotes per day. Over time, storing and accessing the data had become costly and difficult. In addition, older records had to be deleted due to various technical restrictions around capacity and storage. Only sub-sets of data were available at any given time for analysis, limiting visibility into trends and patterns impacting the business.

Solution

Moving to a big data analytics platform enabled Markerstudy to aggregate, store, correlate and analyse terabytes of data cost effectively, while tapping into new data sources that were previously unavailable. While the initial focus was to enhance the performance of its centralised rating portal, Markerstudy expanded the use of its big data analytics platform to encompass other areas of its operations, including risk and underwriting, pricing, claims fraud and customer insight. Data is now analysed from 12 different internal and external sources including policy and claim systems, adjuster notes, social feeds, weather data, traffic patterns and third-party data such as Experian.

Results

In terms of performance gains, the company is now able to process 100 per cent of its quote data within seconds, compared to the previous environment where only 5 per cent of the quote data was available in a seven-hour window. Markerstudy now ingests over 20,000 messages per second, which is more than 50 times the volume that was ingested previously.

Better fraud detection and prevention at the point of quote has enabled Markerstudy to reduce claim costs by £5 million. The company has also seen a 60 per cent reduction in fraudulent applications. In terms of cost savings by moving to a big data analytics platform, it has seen a 20 per cent annual operational cost saving on rate updates, which previously had to be done on 15 different systems.

DATA STRATEGIES

It might be argued that access to more data gives people more ability to make the data say what they want, as in the case of data around which there are conflicting interests such as political campaigns and so on. Another argument is that collecting and storing more data opens up even more opportunities for that information to be used inappropriately or in ways that may impact upon privacy and security.

However, if you're looking to make sense of data by uncovering insights to support any of the board-level use cases that we've discussed, the general rule of thumb for analytics is that 'more actually is more'. Having access to more data simply gives you a more complete picture of your environment and whatever it is you want to observe, analyse or even predict. The key questions are what types of additional data do you need, and how can you uncover the patterns?

In most cases, there are four types of additional data you can tap into (see Figure 10.1):

- historical data;
- real-time data;
- more frequent or higher-resolution data;
- new sources of data.

If you think about your current data sources, for example, you can tap into more historical data, more real-time data, and more frequent or higher-resolution data (that is, at a higher sampling rate such as every hour instead of every day for example), so that's three additional ways you can enhance what you're currently collecting where it makes sense to do so. The types of data we're talking about might include time series data such as stock trades, video surveillance, weather data, sales data, real-time feeds from intelligent sensors and so on.

The fourth option is to tap into additional data sources, which may provide additional insights either individually or in combination with your current data sources. The ability to 'connect the dots' is a great way to summarise this aspect and, in the context of national security, it has been highlighted in several government testimonies, including the heads of various government intelligence agencies.

Figure 10.1 Four options for tapping into additional data from new and existing sources

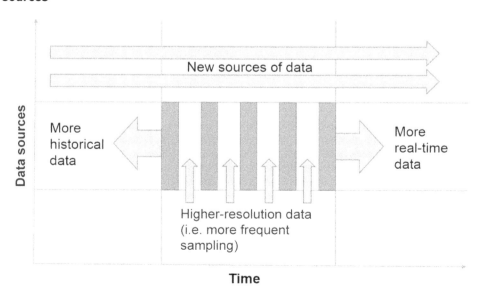

Typical additional data sources may be structured or unstructured feeds that help to uncover patterns and provide additional insights. The typical example here is obviously feeds from social media, which help to provide input on customer sentiment, but which could additionally be leveraged for aspects such as uncovering new product or service opportunities, operational efficiency improvements, market pricing dynamics and customer satisfaction.

Historical data

For every business scenario, your needs will vary, and you'll want to carefully pick and choose between the various options listed above. For example, if we look at historical data, in financial services, access to more historical data can give analysts more information to feed into their predictive models. In health care, electronic health records are capturing massive amounts of clinical data that can be mined for information to improve preventative care and disease treatment.

For the typical enterprise, this storage of historical data raises important questions about how much data to keep and how much may be useful and relevant for future needs. An additional issue, related to backward compatibility, is ensuring that the historical data is stored appropriately so it can be easily accessed in the future. Vint Cerf, Google's Vice President and Chief Internet Evangelist, has highlighted this issue, noting that 'backward compatibility is very hard to preserve over very long periods of time'.[8]

Fortunately, a number of innovative solutions are appearing for long-term digital data storage, including the so-called 'superman memory crystals' invented at the University of Southampton in the UK. By using nanostructured glass, scientists at the university have been able to save digital copies of major documents from human history, including the Universal Declaration of Human Rights and the Magna Carta, which could survive the human race and last for billions of years. The technique uses an ultrafast laser to write data to five-dimensional (5D) storage with 'unprecedented properties including 360 TB/disc data capacity, thermal stability up to 1,000°C and virtually unlimited lifetime at room temperature'.[9] In fact, the storage lifetime is up to 13.8 billion years at an even hotter 190°C. The 5D storage is achieved by using tiny physical structures called 'nanogratings' and using reflected light to provide information about the nanograting's orientation, the strength of the light it reflects and its three-dimensional location.[10]

Real-time data

In terms of collecting and analysing more real-time data, this obviously has many scenarios in the public sector (for example, crime prevention, intelligence, traffic flows) and in health care, manufacturing processes and so on. It can also be applied to help improve revenues and operational efficiencies in retail where items such as real-time sentiment analysis, sales analysis and supply chain monitoring can better inform decision makers.

A good example is P&G's business sphere, a visually immersive data environment set up in over 40 locations around the world, which is an 'integration of technology, visualization, and information that enables leaders to drill down into data to get answers in real-time'. The business sphere environment is similar to a 'mission control' type of setting, where individuals are surrounded by a wall of high-definition screens providing real-time information and analytics. According to P&G,

one supply chain example leveraged supply chain sufficiency models to bring together multiple data points, analytics, and visualizations. This resulted in an inventory reduction of 25% and savings of tens of millions of dollars".[11]

More frequent or higher resolution data

When we think about more frequent or higher resolution data, this could be a finer sampling rate in terms of a time series or perhaps a higher resolution graphical (spatial) model. As an example, if you're scheduling work crews on construction sites across a large city such as London or Chicago, having access to more granular weather forecast data may enable you to keep more crews productive in periods of stormy weather by knowing exactly where the weather may be good or bad.

New sources of data

Finally, tapping into additional data sources to connect the dots and glean new insights is the most commonly cited example around big data analytics. It's also perhaps the hardest challenge to solve in terms of knowing what to look for. It's relatively easy to analyse your existing data sources, since you already have those feeds and know how to process and interpret them. With new feeds from multiple data sources, the challenge is in knowing where to connect the dots and what the uncovered patterns may actually be telling you. I'm a strong believer that solving these challenges takes more than data scientists alone – it takes a multi-disciplinary team of IT staff, data scientists and industry domain experts to put in place the right technical underpinnings, including suitable visualisation technologies, and then iteratively analyse and interpret the information.

Hopefully, these four options for tapping into additional data from both new and existing sources may get you thinking about how you might further utilise your existing data in addition to the wealth of new data sources you now have access to.

DATA ARCHITECTURE

Equipped with board-level use cases for big data analytics, and strategies for how to think about exploiting this data in unique new ways, the next step is to craft an architectural approach to transform your existing data infrastructure to enable a truly data-driven enterprise.

A new data infrastructure is necessary because traditional data infrastructures are not designed to support the volume, velocity and variety of big data, and additionally now need to deal with data that is widely dispersed across both traditional and cloud-based environments.

The EDH

One of the first steps to set up the new data infrastructure is to establish an EDH. According to Mr Reilly, moving to an EDH is the key approach by which organisations can become information-centric and tap into the board-level use cases they wish to pursue.

The EDH provides a single place where all the data that your business generates can be easily accessed by any application or any user in a more agile fashion.

If you've come across the term 'enterprise data lake', then the EDH is one particular instance of a data lake. The enterprise data lake is more of a conceptual term, since in reality many customers need multiple EDHs to meet various requirements such as country-specific data privacy laws or to support different data storage and analysis needs in the cloud versus on-premise.

Enterprise data lakes are typically based on Apache Hadoop, leverage the stability, scalability and flexibility features of Hadoop for data management and then couple that with additional enterprise-level features related to security, governance, management, support and a commercial ecosystem that IT organisations require. The EDH provides unlimited storage of data in its original formats and serves as a data staging area for downstream systems.

Integrating the data architecture into the overall IT transformation

As organisations transform their IT environments to support digital business, one of the questions that arises in connection with the data architecture is how to integrate it with other IT environments that may be transforming simultaneously, such as the move to platform business model technologies and architectures, or the move to software-defined data centre technologies and architectures.

According to Mr Reilly, the beauty of building an EDH on top of Hadoop is that the open source nature of Hadoop provides an assurance of longevity and continual innovation. Since the move to an EDH is a decision that will need to last the next 10 to 20 years, a customer who has adopted an open source strategy can benefit from the innovation across the partner ecosystem (in Cloudera's case over 2,400 companies) as well as having the best options for interoperability and integration.

In the subsequent chapters, we'll continue to explore the overall IT transformation and look at the steps organisations can take to optimise their digital infrastructure, learn how to master the digital services lifecycle, and discover how to simultaneously transform both IT and the business so that you can gain early benefits for customers and end users at the same time as IT transforms its own delivery model.

KEY TAKEAWAYS FOR CHAPTER 10

- Information and data are playing a fundamental, yet highly differentiating, role across all aspects of digital transformation. The key board-level use cases for big data analytics include:

  - customer insights;
  - operational insights;
  - risk management insights.

- In addition to specific business benefits within these areas, each of these use cases can be exploited to create new data-driven business models, products and services.

- The general rule of thumb for analytics is that 'more actually is more'. Having access to more data gives you a more complete picture of your environment and whatever it is you want to observe, analyse or even predict. There are four types of additional data you can tap into:

  - historical data;
  - real-time data;
  - more frequent or higher-resolution data;
  - new sources of data.

- An EDH is the key approach by which organisations can become information-centric and tap into the board-level use cases they wish to pursue. The EDH provides a single place where all the data that your business generates can be easily accessed by any application or any user in a more agile fashion.

11 OPTIMISING DIGITAL INFRASTRUCTURE AND SIMPLIFYING MANAGEMENT

> In the new world, it is not the big fish which eats the small fish, it's the fast fish which eats the slow fish.
> Klaus Schwab, Founder and Executive Chairman, World Economic Forum[1]

Digital transformation is about a lot more than your front-end digital customer experience. It requires a business-critical IT infrastructure on the back-end as well. In the previous chapter, we saw the importance of implementing new data infrastructures to deal with the 3Vs of big data and the strategic role of EDHs in supporting board-level use cases for big data analytics. Another vital element in digital infrastructure has clearly been the move to cloud computing and everything-as-a-service.

Over the years, the agility and cost savings benefits of moving to the cloud have been so compelling that many organisations have experienced 'rogue IT', where business units procure cloud-based applications and services outside the traditional channel of working through their IT organisation. If 'rogue IT' is what happens when business doesn't speak to IT, then 'rogue digital' may be what happens if the CDO doesn't speak to the CIO or vice versa.

To implement a next-generation digital infrastructure, capable of supporting the business for many years ahead, what's needed is a focus on a number of aspects that span the roles of both the CDO and the CIO: a focus on the customer experience across all new digital channels, processes and devices; a focus on business-critical 'interactions' as well as 'transactions'; a focus on new forms of business-critical infrastructure, such as cloud service brokers and software-defined principles, to cost-effectively deliver increased service levels; and a focus on new approaches to provide enterprise-grade security against today's emerging threats.

To embark on a digital transformation journey strategically, as opposed to an ad hoc, piecemeal approach, it's important to think about the highly virtualised, highly distributed, data centre of the future and the key capabilities that will need to be in place from an enterprise IT perspective. After all, although a rising percentage of data centre workloads are migrating to the cloud, the fact is that we'll be living in a hybrid IT environment for many years to come and it will be comprised of a mix of traditional data centre, outsourced, and public and private cloud deployment environments supported by a multitude of providers.

For pioneering CIOs, the challenge is therefore to support the CDO's digital transformation objectives in a highly agile, flexible, manageable and secure manner by putting in place an innovative IT infrastructure that can serve as a foundational platform. This platform will need to blend the 'old' with the 'new'. It will need to retain the business-critical capabilities of the traditional data centre, yet expand this to support modern, digitally transformed business processes and their associated users, applications and devices.

In this chapter, we'll therefore take a look at the emerging requirements for the data centre of the future, the enabling technologies that can be applied to optimise this infrastructure and to simplify its management, key components of the future data centre services and executive recommendations for implementation.

EMERGING REQUIREMENTS FOR THE FUTURE DATA CENTRE

To get to the vision of the data centre of the future, where growth-oriented digital transformation initiatives are enabled by an innovative IT infrastructure that serves as a highly agile foundational platform, CIOs are faced with four key emerging requirements:

- **Agile and cost-effective infrastructure to deliver increased business-critical service levels** – cost-effectively deliver increased business-critical service levels so that the enterprise can scale up to support an increasing number of business-critical applications and processes coming online.

- **Flexible assembly and dynamic execution of digital services from multiple cloud providers** – support the flexible assembly and dynamic execution of digital services, often distributed across multiple cloud providers, to react rapidly to new digital initiatives and fast-changing business needs.

- **Integrated, data-driven view of service management across the enterprise** – achieve an integrated view of service management across the enterprise, to deliver services more efficiently and effectively, and free up time and resources to focus on strategic initiatives.

- **Enterprise-grade security against today's emerging threats** – implement enterprise-grade security against today's emerging threats so that the business value of new digital initiatives can be quickly realised and not delayed.

We'll explore each of these areas in depth to understand exactly why they're having an impact on the vision for the data centre of the future.

1. Agile and cost-effective infrastructure to deliver increased business-critical service levels

With the exploding number of applications and business processes becoming digitised across the enterprise, one of the first requirements for CIOs is to seek out cost-effective approaches to scale up and support these new initiatives while maintaining business-critical service levels.

In recent years, a large part of this cost-effectiveness challenge has been addressed by 'cloud first' initiatives and the strategy of moving to a hybrid cloud model, where workloads are executed on a variety of deployment environments (such as public cloud, private cloud and traditional in-house or outsourced data centres) based on their particular needs such as financial, performance and security requirements.

Today, it's estimated that anywhere from 40 to 60 per cent of enterprise applications are deemed mission critical. As more and more applications become mission critical, CIOs are looking to move to a more homogeneous foundation for their data centres so they can run these applications more cost-effectively and replace their former costly and proprietary systems, which also required highly specialised skill sets.

End-user expectations related to application service levels have increased to the point where there is little tolerance for downtime of any kind. In addition, IT-related threats rank as the top threats to business continuity. For example, a recent report published by the Business Continuity Institute, in association with the British Standards Institution, revealed that IT-related threats are continuing to provide the greatest concern for organisations, ranking above other threats such as natural disasters, security incidents and industrial disputes.[2]

With the expanding scope of business-critical applications, and rising expectations for business-critical service levels, organisations need to find approaches that allow them to meet these new requirements in a cost-effective manner; to do 'more with less', without having to increase their data centre footprint or labour requirements.

2. Flexible assembly and dynamic execution of digital services from multiple cloud providers

The second emerging requirement for the data centre of the future is to support the flexible assembly and dynamic execution of digital services. In many cases, digital business applications and processes need to be provisioned and executed on the fly, often drawing from software components and specialised services located across multiple providers in the public or private cloud, as well as the corporate data centre. Much like an orchestra, this requires careful arrangement to assemble the required elements in the correct manner.

As the data centre evolves and becomes ever-more virtualised, the types of digital services and their related deployment environments are getting more and more diverse. This is necessitating new techniques for managing and brokering these services. For example, the cloud service brokerage market, whereby software helps to integrate and aggregate services from diverse cloud providers, is projected to double in size over four years to become a $160 billion market by 2018.[3] This means an increasing percentage of cloud services are being consumed via internal or external cloud service brokerages rather than directly. In terms of assembling services, hybrid clouds must now support static, deployment, event and dynamic service composition.[4]

The concepts of cloud management and cloud service brokering are key techniques that can help to deliver this flexible management of multiple cloud providers and orchestration of digital services in a more manageable and automated manner for data centre operations.

While cloud management and brokering is one critical aspect – to create an efficient 'digital assembly line' to support rapid provisioning of digital services – organisations will need to drive further automation into the data centre as a whole. They can do this by adopting a software-defined approach that includes not just a virtualisation layer, but an integration layer leveraging service-oriented architectures (SOA) and APIs, a cloud service management and brokerage layer, an SDN layer and a fabric-based architecture.

3. Integrated, data-driven view of service management across the enterprise

The third emerging requirement for the data centre of the future is to achieve an integrated view of service management across the enterprise, to deliver services more efficiently and effectively, and free up time and resources to focus on strategic initiatives. Service management refers to the discipline of designing, delivering, managing and improving the way business and IT services are used within an organisation.[5]

Today, the emphasis of service management is as much on the demand side (that is, the level of service from the view of the customer or end user) as it is on the supply side (that is, the service provider, such as the infrastructure and operations organisation). Service management is also evolving from its roots in IT service management (ITSM), into business service management (that is, supporting many departments beyond IT such as facilities, field service, finance and HR), and now digital service management (that is, supporting all forms of digitally delivered services) as organisations seek to manage and improve their ever-expanding digital services. Today's focus on service management also extends to managing a broad array of business and IT service providers and integrating them into an end-to-end set of services that meet business requirements. In the UK, this discipline is termed service integration and management or SIAM.

The ability of IT organisations to manage the virtual data centre from end to end with a single service management dashboard is becoming increasingly important due to the constantly evolving nature of today's highly virtualised, highly distributed data centres and the needs of today's highly mobile workforce. Self-service portals are being used to let users submit service requests, log issues and track progress to get requests solved quickly and efficiently. A single service management dashboard provides service owners with improved access to data and enhanced visibility required for more effective service delivery and lower total ownership costs.

The overall goal is to boost productivity and increase efficiency by delivering services faster through workflow automation; consolidating redundant systems; automating manual, repetitive tasks; standardising service processes; and offering superior self-service capabilities to end users.

4. Enterprise-grade security against today's emerging threats

The final requirement for the data centre of the future is that CIOs need to be able to configure and manage security in a software-defined manner with global company-wide policies. The reason this is important is that most present-day security controls do not provide sufficient protection against today's emerging threats and take too long to manually re-configure when new vulnerabilities are detected.

Traditional 'perimeter-based' security models have been rendered ineffective by two evolving forces: the increasing sophistication, frequency and scale of cybercrime, and the rapid adoption of new, disruptive IT technologies. In addition, the next wave of emerging trends, such as the IoT, wearable devices and SDNs, are eroding this perimeter model even further.

Today, 80 per cent of security spend is still going on firewalls, intrusion detection systems (IDS) and anti-virus solutions, despite these only being effective for 30 per cent of threats.[6] Today's cyber threats have a lot more to do with vulnerabilities exposed by technologies such as mobile, social and cloud. Perimeter-based strategies are now 20 years old and today's cybercriminals can simply go straight to the end user to get their data. As an example, according to Gartner, cloud and mobile implementations are already starting to bypass the security perimeter. By 2018, 25 per cent of corporate data traffic will bypass perimeter security (up from 4 per cent today) and flow directly from mobile devices to the cloud.[7]

Securing against emerging threats, including securing technologies such as social, mobile and cloud, also impacts time to market. According to the World Economic Forum, estimated delays addressing cyber risks associated with technologies such as cloud, IoT, mobile and social, ranged from 11 months for cloud to 3 months for social computing.[8] To prevent unnecessary delays in realising the benefits of these various technology enablers, therefore, requires a larger percentage of spend to be redirected here versus perimeter security.

A totally new approach to cyber security is required that will ultimately enable the transformative benefits and usage of these enabling technologies without increasing the risk of sensitive data loss and jeopardising business-critical operations. Securing against emerging threats also necessitates an ability to configure and manage security in a more automated, software-defined manner with global company-wide policies so that new technologies can be adopted, implemented and secured efficiently without impacting time to market.

IMPLEMENTING THE FUTURE DATA CENTRE

Having reviewed the emerging requirements for the data centre of the future, we'll now take a look at the enabling technologies that can be applied to optimise data centre infrastructure and to simplify its management, key components of the future data centre services, and executive recommendations for implementation.

Enabling technologies for the future data centre

In Chapter 4, we discussed how, as the IT industry moves into the next wave of corporate IT, the data centre of the future needs to become the workhorse that hosts, manages and delivers this compelling new experience for customers, partners and employees. We discussed how, just as the data centre needs to deliver a new generation of SMAC-enabled applications to digital consumers, and to the digital workforce, it also needs to embrace the changes occurring within data centre technologies themselves. We saw that there have been a number of technology innovations relating to data centre operations and management that have helped to optimise data centre processes as shown in Table 11.1.

Table 11.1 Enabling technologies for the future data centre

Technology enabler	Description
Fabric computing architectures	By adopting a fabric-based architecture, organisations can gain the agility and flexibility of shared resource pools such as compute, network and storage. This helps to avoid data centre sprawl, where each business-critical application used to have its own dedicated physical server, and helps to speed deployments and reduce costs.
Software-defined principles	By adopting software-defined principles and applying them to the management of applications, infrastructure and even security, organisations can implement a single, software-defined management approach across all environments and eliminate the need for many time-consuming, labour-based activities such as network and firewall configuration.
SDDC	The concept of software-defined principles has given rise to SDNs as well as the broader concept of the SDDC where compute, network and storage resources are all software defined.
SIAM	By adopting SIAM tools and approaches, organisations can better manage a broad array of business and IT service providers and integrate them into an end-to-end set of services that meet business requirements.
Cloud management	By adopting advanced automation tools that extend across their hybrid cloud infrastructures, organisations can reduce their operational and infrastructure costs, and selectively run workloads in the infrastructure best suited to meet their financial, performance and security requirements.
Data management	By adopting an EDH, organisations can enable a single place where all the data that their business generates can be easily accessed by any application or any user in a more agile, timely and cost-effective fashion.
Security	By adopting security technologies that focus on micro-segmentation as opposed to securing the traditional 'perimeter', organisations can change the security paradigm and take a more dynamic, software-defined approach that enhances overall manageability.

For the CIO and data centre manager, it's about taking advantage of the cost and agility benefits of these emerging platform and infrastructural technologies so that they can retain the business-critical capabilities of their traditional data centres, yet expand this to support modern, digitally transformed business processes and their associated users, applications and devices.

Key components of the future data centre

It's important to look at the future data centre through the lens of five key service layers that support digital business initiatives by providing user experience services, application services, infrastructure services, security services and management services (see Figure 11.1).

When the future data centre requirements are implemented via the technology enablers outlined above, we see that they fit within five key service layers as follows:

1. **User experience layer** – provides end-to-end management across all new digital processes, channels and devices including mobile environment management, for a personalised, consistent and contextually relevant experience.

2. **Application services layer** – provides modernised services to support digital business requirements with social- and mobile-enablement, delivered via the cloud, with powerful analytics to deliver unique value propositions tailored to end-user needs and interests, preferences and behaviours.

3. **Infrastructure layer** – provides improved service levels, agility and flexibility via cloud computing platforms, cloud service brokerages, fabric computing architectures, software-defined principles and EDHs.

4. **Security layer** – provides the new approaches required for improved cyber security against today's emerging threats with flexible, impenetrable perimeters for data protection and security.

5. **Management layer** – provides a single, software-defined management capability across all environments – including applications, infrastructure and security – for agile and flexible management across the highly virtualised, distributed data centre.

Recommendations for the future data centre

We'll now explore the core areas pertinent to the future, SDDC by looking at infrastructure services, security services and management services.

Infrastructure services

You might think the increased scope for what needs business-critical support will create ever-increasing costs for IT. Fortunately, as business-critical application and workload requirements increase, CIOs are able to employ a number of enabling technologies to their advantage to expand their business-critical footprint and elevate service levels, while carefully managing costs. On-premise data centres can be modernised to utilise cost-effective Windows and Linux platforms and take advantage of cloud technology

Figure 11.1 Key components of digital infrastructure in terms of software-driven service layers

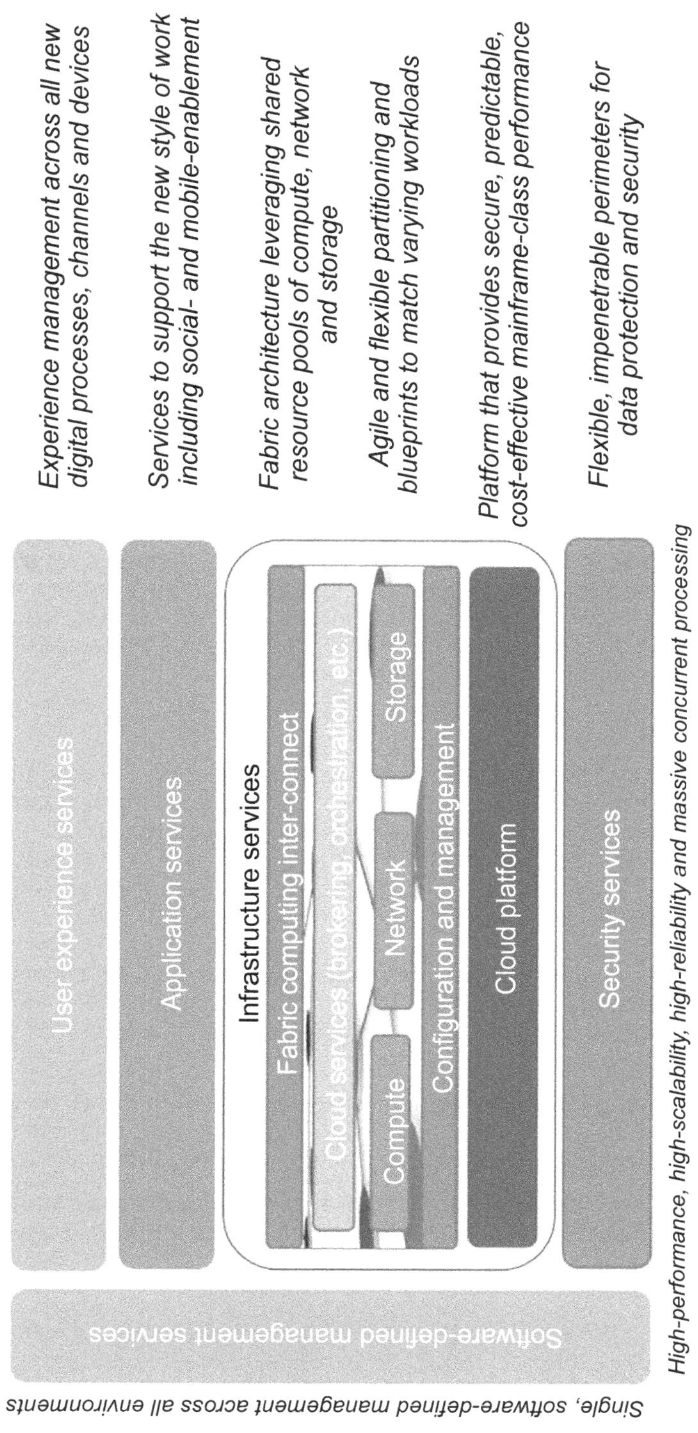

Experience management across all new digital processes, channels and devices

Services to support the new style of work including social- and mobile-enablement

Fabric architecture leveraging shared resource pools of compute, network and storage

Agile and flexible partitioning and blueprints to match varying workloads

Platform that provides secure, predictable, cost-effective mainframe-class performance

Flexible, impenetrable perimeters for data protection and security

User experience services

Application services

Infrastructure services

Fabric computing inter-connect

Cloud services (brokering, orchestration, etc.)

Compute

Network

Storage

Configuration and management

Cloud platform

Security services

Software-defined management services

Single, software-defined management across all environments

High-performance, high-scalability, high-reliability and massive concurrent processing

to reduce data centre footprints and increase virtualisation and partitioning. In this manner, CIOs can deliver improved service levels, but at a more effective price point and with more flexibility to scale up and down on demand.

Traditionally, mission-critical applications have had to run on expensive UNIX and proprietary environments, which required specialised IT skill sets that were very different from the rest of the data centre. Fabric-based platforms and infrastructure, coupled with Windows and Linux operating systems, can be utilised to deliver previously unattainable combinations of cost-effective power, scalability, predictability, performance and security to support business-critical applications on low-cost, industry standard processors.

In addition, cloud computing can be utilised to reduce costs and improve agility and time to market by moving to a hybrid enterprise model where application workloads are placed on the most appropriate deployment environment (for example, public cloud, internal private cloud, hosted private cloud, outsourced or traditional environments) based upon their specific needs.

It is also important to support the agile assembly and dynamic execution of digital services. To create an efficient 'digital assembly line' to support rapid provisioning of digital services, organisations will need to drive further automation into the data centre and adopt a software-defined approach that includes not just a virtualisation layer, but an integration layer (leveraging SOA and APIs), a cloud service brokerage layer, a software-defined network layer and a fabric-based architecture.

Security services

Security is a key attribute that must be pervasive across the entire environment. A new 'zero-trust' (that is, trust no one) deeply embedded security approach, taking the inside-out view, is required to protect information and data across today's highly diverse device types, virtualised applications and distributed infrastructures. Organisations must assume that cybercriminals will penetrate their perimeter, and prepare to protect their critical assets in several key ways:

- **By providing advanced data protection to all critical data assets, both at rest and in motion** – implement enterprise- or even defence-grade encryption together with techniques such as micro-segmentation to secure data at rest and in motion.

- **By preventing lateral movement of malware within the IT environment** – segregate data and transactions inside the network so only those with access know the transaction is occurring, making it undetectable to everyone else.

- **By protecting external IT assets such as cloud infrastructure, mobile devices and the IoT** – for example in the cloud arena, secure and isolate communication between virtual resources in a multi-tenant environment to prevent theft or misuse of data within a tenant and between tenants.

- **By reducing the attack surface to inhibit more sophisticated forms of cyberattack** – cloak servers and other computer or device entry points running sensitive applications or storing private information, making them undetectable to unauthorised users.

One of the key techniques to address all these requirements is micro-segmentation. This is a security technique that essentially ring-fences high-value data and assets, located either within the data centre or external to the traditional security perimeter, by providing protection to specific data, workloads, applications, devices or machines in specifically defined zones. The default approach for micro-segmentation is to trust no one, so the entire mechanism is based on denying all communication unless specifically allowed.[9] This helps to ensure protection from the lateral movement of advanced persistent threats and malware that may have already breached the traditional security perimeter and be already operating inside the IT environment.

Micro-segmentation offers a fine-grained approach to implementing security policies, so it can be focused on the most high-value or highly sensitive sets of data, applications and devices – wherever they reside. It is an agile, cost-effective approach to security since the security policies for micro-segmentation can be centrally managed and software-defined to provide a highly adaptive defence posture.

In addition, by coupling micro-segmentation with threat intelligence from security analytics, organisations can actively seek out threats and apply real-time enforcement. Advanced predictive analysis of data coming from security information and event management and other systems can feed the threat intelligence into a real-time enforcement engine, which can then communicate with the micro-segmentation technology to dynamically change its policies. This can help to isolate and quarantine the malware and limit its movement.

Management services

By implementing a single, software-defined management capability across all service layers in the data centre – including the user experience layer, applications, infrastructure and security – organisations can ensure their business-critical operations can be rapidly configured and re-configured, and also seamlessly managed and monitored with visibility across the entire end-to-end infrastructure.

The software-defined management capability should also extend across all deployment environments in the highly virtualised, distributed data centre – including public cloud, internal and hosted private cloud, outsourced and traditional environments.

Integrated service management approaches can be utilised to span all end points, applications and infrastructure with a set of consolidated and customised service views coupled with powerful analytics to generate actionable insights from systems data. This allows service management organisations to foresee impending outages or predict shifts in user demand for a more pro-active approach to service delivery.

The use of software-defined principles means that organisations can 'wire once' and avoid recurring, time-consuming, labour-based activities such as network and firewall configuration. For most effective manageability, it's important to look beyond software-defined networks and storage and towards emerging areas such as software-defined security in order to automate as much as possible up and down the entire IT stack.

Summary

Today's business-critical infrastructure and operations need to serve as a foundation for future needs and be aware of the new and constantly evolving scope of business-critical computing. This requires re-thinking process scope, application scope, service levels and business continuity plans, and risk management strategies – all in the context of today's IT operations and data centres running low-cost, industry standard platforms to 'achieve more for less'.

So doing will help digital transformation initiatives avoid 'rogue digital' and achieve the best of both worlds in terms of supporting the business-critical capabilities of traditional data centres together with the new demands of digital business models, processes, products and services. To achieve this bi-modal capability, the CDO and CIO will need to work in close collaboration to harness the full potential of their respective organisations.

KEY TAKEAWAYS FOR CHAPTER 11

- To implement a next-generation digital infrastructure, capable of supporting the business for many years ahead, what's needed is a focus on a number of aspects that span the roles of both the CDO and the CIO:

  - The digital customer experience across all new digital channels, processes and devices.

  - Business-critical 'interactions' as well as 'transactions'.

  - New forms of business-critical infrastructure.

  - New approaches to enterprise-grade security.

- Emerging requirements for the data centre of the future include:

  - agile and cost-effective infrastructure to deliver increased business-critical service levels;

  - flexible assembly and dynamic execution of digital services from multiple cloud providers;

  - an integrated data-driven view of service management across the enterprise;

  - enterprise-grade security against today's emerging threats.

- CIOs and data centre managers can take advantage of the cost and agility benefits of new platform and infrastructural technologies so that they can retain the business-critical capabilities of their traditional data centres, yet expand to support digitally transformed business processes and their associated users, applications and devices.

PART IV
ROADMAP – TAKING AN AGILE JOURNEY TO
THE NEW PLATFORM ECOSYSTEM

12 MASTERING THE DIGITAL SERVICES LIFECYCLE AND SPEEDING TIME TO MARKET

Speed is the new currency of business.

Marc R. Benioff, Chairman and CEO, Salesforce[1]

Mastery of digital services is going to become a key competency for organisations to grow their business and build sustainable competitive advantage in the years ahead. It's no longer sufficient to have an innovative set of products or services; you have to be a master of how you design, develop, deploy, manage and continually evolve your digital services as well.

In this chapter, we'll explore how organisations can master the digital services lifecycle and look at the set of innovative service delivery techniques that are becoming essential to developing an end-to-end capability that spans design and development all the way to deployment and management.

Even if your company delivers physical goods, digital services – in the form of both inter-actions and transactions – will likely be a growing part of your business both now and in the years ahead. In 2015, the service sector was close to 65 per cent of gross domestic product (GDP) worldwide[2] and according to McKinsey, 'services are expected to account for about three-quarters of global growth over the coming decade'.[3]

If we look at interactions, digital interfaces and channels are likely the primary way your customer engages with your business. This has benefits for both the customer and your organisation. For example, digital customer care ('eCare') studies, such as that conducted by McKinsey, who looked at the telecommunications industry, have clearly shown that eCare can both lower costs as well as enhance customer satisfaction.[4] They found that solutions such as digital chat amounted to 54 per cent of a call centre's cost when compared to voice, and that customer satisfaction was 19 percentage points higher for those who took a purely digital customer service journey compared to a purely 'traditional' journey.

If we look at transactions – that is, revenue opportunities – the product purchase is a one-time transaction, but, as we've seen previously, the services associated with the product provide the opportunity for continual customer engagement and annuity revenues.

Just look at the connected home for example. A home security system may be just a few hundred pounds for the physical equipment, but the monthly service fees for monitoring, remote viewing on mobile devices and cloud storage of camera footage provide a perpetual revenue stream. The Nike+ running app and ecosystem is another oft-cited example of a suite of services wrapped around a physical product.

Of course, the service-wrapping concept also extends into industry and B2B scenarios, such as the Industrial Internet and Industry 4.0. The data that swirls around these factories, fleets, machines, equipment and products can be collected, aggregated, processed, analysed and ultimately monetised in a wide range of emerging scenarios.

The upshot of all this is that the ability to design, develop, deploy and manage digital services – and do this with tremendous agility and at high levels of sophistication and scale – is going to be a critical capability for organisations that wish to become, or even remain, digital leaders within their industries.

As we saw in Chapter 8, with digital business comes the expectation of intelligent, personalised and contextualised services that can be provided to customers, which are rapidly re-designed or enhanced as business needs dictate. In addition, the service itself may need to dynamically adjust based on the customer's context, environmental parameters, business exceptions or other changing business conditions.

According to Gartner's predictions for IT organisations and users,

> By 2017, 70 percent of successful digital business models will rely on deliberately unstable processes designed to shift as customer needs shift.[5]

Since the processes are manifested via software, these software services will therefore need to be able to dynamically adjust according to customer needs.

So while the familiar SMAC technologies provide the foundational building blocks, together with emerging building blocks such as the IoT, there is also a need for innovative service delivery techniques and approaches to keep pace with digital business.

You can think of this as the 'what' and the 'how'. Just as a magician has valuable props (the 'what') essential to his performance, he also needs to perfect his sleight of hand (the 'how').

If you think about these innovative service delivery techniques essential for digital service mastery, they break out into elements you need internally for IT efficiency and elements you need externally for the digital customer experience. In some cases, excellence in one area helps to inform and improve the other.

Taking a lifecycle perspective, in the digital services lifecycle, the idea is to accelerate digital service development and deployment, make services agile, scalable and available on demand, automate extensively, personalise and contextualise for the customer experience, and manage holistically.

Table 12.1 provides a listing of the essential innovative service delivery techniques and approaches that are required for digital services mastery and their corresponding benefits to both IT and the business. These techniques start with agile development and methodologies, and progress through the service delivery lifecycle to ongoing digital service management.

Table 12.1 Innovative tools and approaches for digital services mastery

Innovative service delivery technique or approach	IT benefit	Business benefit
Agile development and methodologies	Accelerates application development with sprints producing new code releases in days or weeks compared to months or years in the traditional 'waterfall' approach.	Enables digital services to be rapidly iterated and improved, based on customer feedback.
DevOps	Eliminates functional silos between application development and deployment groups.	Enables a faster and more reliable transition of digital services into production.
As-a-service infrastructure	Reduces IT cost with cloud-based infrastructure that can be scaled up or down based on workload.	Provides digital services that are agile, scalable and available on demand.
Intelligent automation	Reduces IT cost and complexity by reducing dependence on labour-based processes, and optimises service efficiency.	Delivers more efficient, real-time digital services by removing manual bottlenecks.
Personas and context	Provides IT staff with information, applications and analytics more specific to their roles to make them more productive and to improve decision making.	Personalises and contextualises services for the digital customer experience.
Digital service management	Helps to manage 'shadow IT' by managing IT services across the entire environment with a real-time view into service requests, status and outages.	Provides visibility into business service performance, so organisations can continually monitor the quality of the customer experience according to the business parameters that are important to them.

With this perspective in mind, here are six key questions to ask of your current digital initiatives to see where your organisation lies in terms of digital services mastery and what new techniques and approaches may be able to lend additional, even transformative, value:

1. **With an envisioned business model or process at hand, how quickly can you develop it via software?** With today's pace of innovation, time to market is critical. Techniques here include agile development and methodologies, and while this is not a new trend, it's certainly gaining traction as a way to keep up with the volume of requests from the business and the need to deliver results rapidly and iteratively. As such, digital business provides the 'burning platform' to make agile approaches more important now than ever.

2. **How quickly and reliably can you move digital services into production?** The idea is to speed digital service deployment to place applications into production as rapidly as they're developed. Techniques here include DevOps, for a faster and more reliable transition into production, and web-scale IT, for scalability. By way of definition, web-scale IT is an architectural approach, adopted from the practices of large cloud services providers, that emphasises design for resilience, scale and performance. Business-critical infrastructure is vital here as well.

3. **How responsive is your IT infrastructure to dynamically changing business conditions?** The idea is to make services agile and flexible, with on-demand consumption and support for rapid changes to business rules. Techniques here include software-defined principles, including the concept of the SDDC, so that configuration changes can be applied via software as opposed to time-consuming manual tasks such as network and firewall configuration.

4. **How automated are your digital services?** The idea is to reduce IT cost and complexity by reducing dependence on labour-based processes and optimising service efficiency. Techniques here include robotic process automation and machine learning. While physical robots and drones gain the majority of media attention, software robots are at present the unsung heroes and are already delivering significant results.

5. **How compelling is your digital customer experience?** The idea here is clearly to delight and engage customers with compelling digital experiences so they become (or remain) loyal customers and you can gain a sustainable competitive advantage. Techniques include personalisation, context, analytics-driven insights (into customer preferences, needs and interests), natural interfaces, user interface design, multi-channel support and much more.

6. **How well can you manage your services and gain visibility into digital service performance?** The idea is to simplify service management and to be able to manage holistically across all your digital channels. With 'shadow IT' on the rise, and with today's hybrid IT environments, this is a far more difficult challenge than might be imagined. Techniques here include ITSM tools and approaches such as SIAM that help you to manage IT services, but also help you to manage higher-level business services as well, so that you can continually monitor the quality of your customer experience according to the business parameters that are important to them.

Progress in these six areas will help you to build your organisation's mastery of the digital services lifecycle in terms of the digital touch points, interactions and transactions with your customers. With this competency at hand, and with continual improvement, your organisation will be well poised to compete in the digital world in the years to come.

KEY TAKEAWAYS FOR CHAPTER 12

- Mastery of digital services is going to become a key competency for organisations to grow their business and build sustainable competitive advantage in the years ahead. It's no longer sufficient to have an innovative set of products or services; you have to be a master of how you design, develop, deploy, manage and continually evolve your digital services as well.

- So while the familiar SMAC technologies provide the foundational building blocks, together with emerging building blocks such as the IoT, there is also a need for innovative service delivery techniques and approaches to keep pace with digital business.

- You can think of this as the 'what' and the 'how'. Just as a magician has valuable props (the 'what') essential to his performance, he also needs to perfect his sleight of hand (the 'how').

- Taking a lifecycle perspective, in the digital services lifecycle, the idea is to accelerate digital service development and deployment, make services agile, scalable and available on demand, automate extensively, personalise and contextualise for the customer experience, and manage holistically.

- Innovative techniques and approaches for digital services mastery include agile, DevOps, as-a-service infrastructure, intelligent automation, personas and context, and digital service management.

13   THE AGILE JOURNEY TO THE NEW PLATFORM

It is not the strongest of the species that survives, nor the most intelligent that survives. It is the one that is the most adaptable to change.

Adapted from Charles Darwin[1]

In terms of digital transformation initiatives, there's often a lot of talk in terms of strategy and less emphasis on practical execution. Everyone wants to advise the CEO and the board, but these discussions often only take the conversation so far.

So how should an organisation think beyond the strategy and get to transformative execution and outcomes? It's important to develop an approach that can span this divide between strategy and execution so that once the transformation objectives have been selected, there's a clear path to a unified architectural approach and subsequent agile execution.

In this chapter we'll explore six steps for digital transformation that you can take to progress from innovative strategy development, to an architectural framework, to practical execution. The steps incorporate everything we've learned so far in this book across the major sections on planning, insight, action and roadmap. In the introduction, we saw how mastering digital business is a function of disruptive technologies, platform business models and digital services mastery – all accelerated by leading practices in corporate innovation:

MASTERING DIGITAL BUSINESS =

> Function of (Disruptive Technologies + Platform Business Models + Digital Services Mastery)

> Accelerated by (Leading Practices in Corporate Innovation)

What we're saying here is that whatever your digital transformation objective, from a business perspective (i.e. 'business-led, not technology-led'), you can get there by following this approach. Each of these elements can be a key enabler to help you achieve your target business outcomes and become a digital business leader.

Now that we're close to the end of our journey in this book, we can pull all this together to see how to execute the vision and roadmap. It all starts by identifying your transformation objectives. This may well be a combination of new business models (Chapter 1), new business processes (Chapter 2), or any of the more specific business objectives we explored across the digital customer experience (Chapter 8), the digital workplace (Chapter 9), insights from analytics (Chapter 10), and optimising digital infrastructure and simplifying management (Chapter 11). These chapters aimed to highlight the art of the possible and to provide some compelling examples from some of today's digital business leaders.

With your transformation objectives in mind, you can then proceed to employ the various technology enablers in the market (Chapter 3), assemble them into a suitable platform architecture and platform business model (Chapter 4), incorporate your mastery of the digital services lifecycle (Chapter 12), and accelerate your journey with leading practices in corporate innovation and a clear understanding of how to best to time your move (Chapters 5–7).

Finally, you'll execute the journey via a series of initiatives that will help you to simultaneously transform both the business and IT so that you can gain early benefits for customers and end users at the same time as IT transforms its own delivery model.

Table 13.1 provides a summary of the six steps for digital transformation, together with some of the key elements and considerations within each step.

Table 13.1 Six steps for digital transformation

Digital transformation step	Key elements and considerations
1. Identify your transformation objectives	Digital transformation strategy, digital transformation focus, investment
2. Study technology enablers in the market	Disruptive technology enablers: SMAC, IoT, intelligent automation, personas and content, cyber security – plus others such as 3D printing and blockchain
3. Envision the future platform for digital business	Platform architectures and business models
4. Master the digital services lifecycle	Digital services mastery: agile, DevOps, as-a-service infrastructure, intelligent automation, personas and context, digital service management
5. Organise for digital business innovation	Innovation management, change management, governance
6. Execute an agile journey to the future platform	Leadership, culture, digital skills: business and IT transformation

So here are six steps for digital transformation, which should help to show how everything comes together, and how you can progress from innovative strategy development, to an architectural framework, to practical execution.

Step 1 – Identify your transformation objectives

Strategy and vision >> digital transformation strategy, digital transformation focus, investment

In terms of identifying your transformation objectives, this step corresponds to the strategy and vision aspect of your digital transformation journey. As you progress from strategy to execution, it's important for the strategy to set the stake in the ground in terms of target business outcomes. Digital business is often discussed solely from the lens of the digital customer experience, but as we've seen, that's only a part of the story – albeit a vital part. In addition to re-thinking and re-designing entire business models, the key desired transformation objectives often map to the following areas:

- Enhancing the digital customer and end-user experience to improve loyalty, revenues, productivity and retention.

- Transforming business processes to reduce costs, improve productivity, integrate supply chain partners and differentiate offerings.

- Deriving insights from analytics to make better decisions, improve efficiencies and gain competitive advantage.

- Optimising infrastructure and operations to improve agility, flexibility and cost-effectiveness.

- Simplifying management to reduce complexity, solve issues before they occur, and gain visibility and control over assets.

Every organisation will have a slightly different set of transformational objectives, with different priorities, but this is a vital first step for organisational alignment. All this should help to inform and refine your overall strategy and vision in terms of your digital transformation strategy, digital transformation focus and investments.

You can refer to the strategic options for business model innovation and the characteristics of digital business processes described in Chapter 2 to help explore your strategic options and develop your strategy and vision. For example, we saw how business models can be re-designed to digitise products and services and to run or participate within industry platforms by tapping into the sharing economy, reshaping value networks and creating new models for monetisation. We also saw how business processes can be re-designed to be experience-centric, automated, simplified, digitised, personalised, dynamic, real time, granular, aggregated and scalable to maximise their value propositions.

Step 2 – Study technology enablers in the market

Technology and capabilities >> disruptive technology enablers

The next step is to be fully aware of, and leverage, the technology enablers in the market. This step, and the following two steps, correspond to the technology and capabilities aspects of your digital transformation journey.

It's important to look beyond the SMAC stack and into the next wave of enablers, including personas and context, intelligent automation including human–machine collaboration, the IoT and, of course, cyber security. As we've seen, advanced cyber security is a key enabler because when emerging technologies are not secure from the start, it creates delays in realising the technology's full business benefits as organisations struggle to implement appropriate security controls.

In addition to these more recent enablers, the core SMAC stack is clearly evolving as well. Mobility is evolving and embracing wearable technologies, and the cloud is evolving and embracing broader concepts such as hybrid IT and SDDCs. These key disruptive technologies now serve as the foundational building blocks – some mature, some emerging – in the new digital business platform ecosystem of on-demand services. Taking a holistic view across all these enablers can help to maximise business benefits and unlock new forms of value in the years ahead.

You can refer to the examples and case studies provided in Chapter 3 to help understand the business value of each technology enabler and how it can be integrated into your overall approach. In addition, you can refer to the three waves of disruptive technology adoption discussed in Chapter 7 to help you best exploit the position of each specific technology for business model transformation (emerging wave), high competitive advantage (differentiating wave) or proven business value (business value wave).

Step 3 – Envision the future platform for digital business

Technology and capabilities >> platform architectures and business models

In terms of technologies and capabilities, this step relates to how you assemble your foundational technology enablers to form digital business platform architectures as well as digital business platform business models.

The new platform can be used as a frame of reference for digital business transformation in terms of the key IT capabilities – both technologies and approaches – needed to support your transformation objectives. In Chapter 3, we discussed six key characteristics of the platform and how the model can help with your planning.

Architecturally, the foundational technology enablers can be utilised to assemble a highly virtualised, highly distributed platform ecosystem of on-demand services. Based on your perspective, you'll select powerful combinations of these technologies to achieve target business outcomes such as enhancing the digital customer experience, transforming the digital workplace, gaining insights from analytics, optimising infrastructure, simplifying management and implementing an adaptive cyber security defence posture. You can refer to Chapter 4 for several real-life examples of these technology combinations in action.

Rather than a monolithic platform, the future platform will consist of an ecosystem of services from best-in-class providers. Foundational services will be selected based upon role-specific (for example, digital manager, application manager, infrastructure manager, IT operations manager) and outcome-oriented needs. Common groupings of pre-integrated services will emerge, such as those provided by EDHs and SDDCs, so that you don't have to do all the assembly yourself.

In terms of practical execution, business managers can therefore select from this palette of options based on their specific needs. For example, by applying the 'technology lever' for the enhancing digital customer experience that we discussed in Chapter 8, we can deliver a new set of capabilities drawing from the 'digital experience essentials' as well as the 'digital experience enhancers'. More broadly, in the case of the digital customer experience, the full set of technology enablers can be envisioned, based on an understanding of the key attributes essential for a world-class experience as we outlined in the DCX Bill of Rights.

In addition to considering the digital business platform architecture, it's also vital to consider the various platform business model opportunities we explored in Chapter 4. You can use the business strategy and IT strategy questions and considerations pertaining to platform business models outlined in the chapter to help plan your approach. At this step along the journey, envisioning the future platform should be as much about your future platform business model as it is about your future platform architecture, and the two operate hand in hand.

Step 4 – Master the digital services lifecycle

Technology and capabilities >> digital services mastery

The next step for IT is to consider the 'how' as well as the 'what'. It's no longer sufficient to have an innovative set of products or services (the 'what'); you have to be a master of how you design, develop, deploy, manage and continually evolve your digital services (the 'how') as well. Mastery of the digital services lifecycle is going to become a key competency for organisations to grow their business and build sustainable competitive advantage in the years ahead.

All in all, there are six key approaches that are shaping how digital services are produced and consumed: agile, DevOps, as-a-service infrastructure, intelligent automation, personas and context, and, finally, digital service management.

Collectively, these capabilities help to accelerate digital service development and deployment, make services available on demand, automate extensively, personalise to specific roles and manage holistically. Progress in these six areas will help you to build your organisation's mastery of the digital services lifecycle in terms of the digital touch points, interactions and transactions with your customers.

You can use the strategic questions posed in Chapter 12 to help assess your current digital initiatives to see where your organisation lies in terms of digital services mastery and what new techniques and approaches may be able to lend additional, even transformative, value. By increasing your organisation's maturity along each of these dimensions you'll be able to continually and rapidly innovate your digital services based on customer and market demands.

Step 5 – Organise for digital business innovation

Process and governance >> innovation management, change management, governance

In terms of organising for digital business innovation, this step corresponds to the process and governance aspect of your digital transformation journey. Some of the key elements include innovation management, change management and governance.

You can use the five critical pillars of innovation management capability outlined in Chapter 5 to help assess your current innovation programme and determine any gaps or improvements needed to ensure you have a robust innovation process that connects into all the appropriate corporate strategy, investment, and product and service development processes.

You can also use the information related to ongoing and event-based ideation presented in Chapter 6 to help ensure your organisation can maximise the innovation potential across your diverse ecosystem of employees, customers, suppliers and partners in a systematic manner and equally be able to mobilise ideation sessions as, where and when opportunities arise. Ongoing idea generation gives you a way to capture ideas from across the organisation whenever they arise, and event-based idea generation gives you a way to take a more targeted approach for specific audiences, goals and objectives, and key focus areas.

In terms of governance, one of the key changes here is that governance now needs to span both the slower-paced, incremental 'business as usual' initiatives as well as the faster-paced, more disruptive 'transformation' initiatives. This doesn't mean that the type of governance and level of governance needs to be identical across both types of initiatives, but that the governance function will need to provide visibility across them both and will need to be more responsive and adaptive to the new pace of change and the frequent sprint cycles inherent in transformation initiatives. These initiatives will most likely be pursing agile and lean approaches to rapidly iterate around new products and services with frequent customer interaction and feedback. Governance programmes will therefore need to adjust some of their cadences related to reporting and metrics to strike the right balance between providing management insight and visibility, while ensuring a lightweight and flexible approach.

In terms of change management, CIOs and business leaders don't have to create entirely new processes, or reinvent the wheel, to execute on digital initiatives. In Chapter 5 we saw that you can use existing corporate funding and corporate innovation mechanisms, but will need to make five critical fine-tuning adjustments to readjust the sights squarely on digital business.

Step 6 – Execute an agile journey to the future platform

People and culture >> leadership, culture, digital skills

In terms of executing on the journey to this new platform, this step corresponds to the people and culture aspect of your digital transformation journey. Some of the key elements include leadership, culture and digital skills. It takes all these elements to successfully make the transformation.

It takes leadership to make innovation and digital transformation a necessity, to enforce behaviours, and to keep programmes chartered and aligned with the external perspective in mind. It takes culture to enable tolerance and receptivity to risk, and to embrace and empower change, and it takes digital skills to do the heavy lifting with a completely new set of tools and techniques.

Whether it's a focus on specific technology enablers such as robotics or the IoT, or a focus on specific techniques such as agile and DevOps, these skills will become more and more critical in the years ahead as organisations invest in scaling up their digital transformation initiatives. These organisations will look to IT professionals to provide compelling, differentiated solutions that enhance the digital customer experience, improve operations, and which can be designed and deployed in an agile manner.

Finally, since business and IT strategy will determine and drive these future skill requirements, organisation-wide capabilities in strategic planning, innovation management, enterprise architecture, programme management and change management will also be essential to pull everything together and execute on the overall transformation. IT professionals will be able to choose whether to go deep in terms of specialising in a specific technology or capability, or whether to go wide in terms of specialising in the broader perspective of how all these elements come together from a strategy and execution standpoint to enable the next generation of digital business solutions.

Finally, when taking the journey to this new platform, it's important to bear in mind that we live in a hybrid IT world. Organisations need to take the journey to the future platform, while supporting and maintaining their existing applications and infrastructure. While some elements may be retired or modernised, other elements may need to co-exist with, and be integrated into, the new platform.

Since IT will be a hybrid environment for quite some time, it will be important to inter-operate across these two divides. In addition, an agile and iterative journey to the future platform can simultaneously optimise infrastructure and simplify management on the back-end (the IT transformation) as well as improve the user experience and transform business processes on the front-end (the business transformation). That way the business can gain early benefits for customers and end users at the same time as IT transforms its own delivery model.

ASSESSING YOUR DIGITAL TRANSFORMATION MATURITY

Since the six steps for digital transformation incorporate all the requisite elements of strategy, people, process and technology, we can use them to develop a simple model to help assess where your organisation sits in terms of digital transformation maturity. Table 13.2 provides the model definitions so you can assess your maturity along each of the six dimensions. To keep the model straightforward, there are three maturity stages, ranging from 'Early' to 'Developing' to 'Maturing'. In the Appendix, you can also find a set of assessment questions that you can take in order to gain a more formal assessment.

You can apply many of the techniques and models presented in the book to help you move from a maturity level of 'Early' to 'Developing', or from 'Developing' to 'Maturing', along any of the six dimensions. For example, if you are currently at the 'Developing' stage in terms of your transformation objectives, you can refer to the various options for business model innovation and for business process re-design described in Step 1 and also in-depth within Chapter 2. You can also advance your mastery of the digital customer experience by referring to the models and case studies in Chapter 8.

As another example, if you are currently at the 'Early' stage in terms of the capabilities of your corporate innovation programme, you can refer to the five critical pillars of innovation management capability described in Chapter 5 as well as the details on event-based and ongoing ideation – including innovation workshops – described in Chapter 6. Likewise, if you are currently at the 'Early' or 'Developing' stage in terms of your digital services mastery, you can refer to the full set of six key capabilities described in Chapter 12, namely agile, DevOps, as-a-service infrastructure, intelligent automation, personas and context, and digital service management.

Table 13.2 Digital transformation maturity model

Digital transformation dimension	Early	Developing	Maturing
Transformation objectives (strategy and vision)	Narrowly targeted transformation objectives	Transforming processes, plus select DCX initiatives	Transforming business models, processes, plus mastery of the DCX
Disruptive technologies (technology and capabilities)	Use of SMAC technologies; primarily perimeter-based security	Use of SMAC, plus select next-generation enablers; moderate security for advanced threats	Use of SMAC, plus strategic set of next-generation enablers; advanced security for advanced threats
Platform business models (technology and capabilities)	No current use of platform business models	Investigating platform business models	Platform business models a core part of digital transformation strategy
Digital services mastery (technology and capabilities)	Mastery of one or two of the key capabilities	Mastery of three or four of the key capabilities	Mastery of five or six of the key capabilities
Organise for digital business innovation (process and governance)	Limited and/ or fragmented innovation programme(s)	Formal innovation programme, but not yet tuned for digital transformation	Continuous and collaborative innovation, fine-tuned for digital transformation
Take the agile journey (people and culture)	Risk adverse; limited digital skills	Risk tolerant; moderate digital skills	Risk receptive; strong digital skills

Digital transformation is clearly a journey, not a destination, so even once you reach maturity across all dimensions, there will be a need for continuous innovation and for continuous and rapid response to change, and to challenges and opportunities as they arise. One of the benefits of moving along the maturity curve is that you can essentially incorporate next-generation skills and capabilities so that agility becomes an intrinsic part of the organisation's operating model. For example:

- Digitally re-designed business processes have a number of characteristics that enable them to trump traditional processes by being experience-centric, automated, simplified, digitised, personalised, dynamic, real time, granular, aggregated and scalable.

- Platform business models enable rapid growth and changes to the ecosystem, since they rely on external producers and consumers to provide the actual – physical or digital – products, services and social currency, so they can scale up and achieve critical mass very quickly.

- Technologies, tools and techniques such as cloud management, EDHs, SDDCs, micro-segmentation and digital service management make IT infrastructure highly agile and cost-effective.

- Techniques such as agile and DevOps enable organisations to iterate rapidly in terms of experimenting with new features, or even entirely new service offerings, and quickly place applications into production once they're developed.

- The overall concept of digital service mastery helps to accelerate digital service development and deployment, makes services agile, scalable and available on demand, automates extensively, personalises and contextualises for the customer experience, and enables them to be managed holistically.

- Innovation programmes that are highly adapted and fine-tuned to support digital transformation initiatives and can embrace the same operating principles – that is, lean, agile, flexible, efficient and more – so they can be executed at speed and at scale.

In the Conclusion, we'll address the digital transformation journey in more detail and discuss what lies ahead for digital transformation as it evolves and becomes ever-more impactful on our lives, our businesses and our societies.

KEY TAKEAWAYS FOR CHAPTER 13

- The six steps for digital transformation provide the steps that you can take to progress from innovative strategy development, to an architectural framework, to practical execution. The steps incorporate everything we've learned so far in this book across our various major sections on planning, insight, action and roadmap.

- The digital transformation maturity model provides a simple model to help assess where your organisation sits in terms of digital transformation maturity. You can apply many of the techniques and models presented in the book to help you to move from a maturity level of 'Early' to 'Developing', or from 'Developing' to 'Maturing', along any of the six dimensions.

- One of the benefits of moving along the maturity curve is that you can essentially incorporate next-generation skills and capabilities so that agility becomes an intrinsic part of the organisation's operating model.

CONCLUSION

> Now this is not the end. It is not even the beginning of the end. But it is, perhaps, the end of the beginning.
>
> Winston Churchill (1942)[1]

Now that we're at the close of our journey to mastering digital business, I hope that the discussion of disruptive technologies, platform business models, digital services mastery and innovation management approaches has helped to shed some light into the practices of today's digital business leaders and provide a glimpse of what's to come in the future, along with some strategic considerations, techniques and approaches that you can apply within your own initiatives.

Digital transformation is a broad subject that requires competency across strategy and vision, people and culture, processes and governance, as well as technology and capabilities as shown in Figure C.1.

Figure C.1 Key pillars of digital transformation

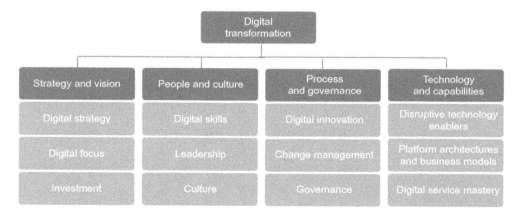

The most successful digital transformation initiatives pay attention to all these areas so that the six steps to digital transformation that we discussed earlier in Chapter 13 can move the organisation seamlessly from strategy to execution. As we saw in our case study about the Mercedes AMG Petronas Formula One Team, a world-leading position doesn't necessarily require world-leading performance in every single domain. It's more a case of being a world leader and innovator in the key areas that matter, and being a fast follower in the rest.

It's my hope this book provides some key insights and advice, as well as motivation, for you to achieve a world-leading position for your organisation, particularly in terms of strategy, innovation, and emerging technologies and capabilities as they pertain to digital transformation. By coupling this with insights from other sources into the 'soft skills' related to leadership, culture, governance and change management, you'll have a powerful combination for success.

So, what lies ahead for digital transformation?

We can be certain that one of the only constants will be change. We can expect change to occur across all the key pillars of digital transformation that we've discussed here: from strategy, to people, process and technology. These may seem like traditional pillars, but there's nothing traditional about them. As we've seen, each pillar involves vastly new approaches when compared to business as usual.

In terms of industry shifts, according to the Global Center for Digital Business Transformation, 40 per cent of companies are at risk of being displaced because they're not equipped for the digital future.[2] I expect we'll continue to see accelerating topple-rates among the Fortune 500 and the FTSE 250, as well as corresponding shifts in industry leaders. We may also see greater separation between digital leaders and laggards – driven by how well they can deliver upon the digital customer experience – as well as more partnerships between industry players and high-tech players as they join forces to create superior offerings and value propositions. These partnerships will be powered by platform- and ecosystem-oriented business models. This will likely generate some of the highest magnitude business disruptions in the years ahead, as platform business models dissolve industry boundaries and hyper-extend the limits of the customer journey from one industry to another.

While SMAC will likely remain the core foundational set of technologies for digital business, we'll see a large number of new technology enablers continue to come into focus as value enhancers within digital business models and processes. The use of the IoT as well as intelligent automation will be megatrends that empower and expand digital business scenarios in the years ahead, as well as raising many issues and challenges along the way in terms of privacy, safety and security.

We'll see a digital workplace that combines the best of what humans and machines have to offer in the form of new human–machine work scenarios. Rather than harsh boundaries between humans and machines, we'll see a converged future where work processes are optimised in two converging directions: instrumentation of human processes and socialisation of machine processes, so the two can work in greater harmony together. Machines will continue to get more social and humans will continue to get more instrumented, all of which will amplify the possibilities.

Much as sleight of hand differentiates magicians who may be using the same props as part of their performance, digital services mastery will become a key point of differentiation for organisations by helping them to innovate their services more rapidly than their competitors and uniquely tailor them for each customer.

We can expect the discipline of innovation management to evolve further as well. In the book, we discussed how innovation needs to go beyond the table-stakes of idea management and provide a complete programme addressing not only the innovation pipeline, but the front-end of the innovation lifecycle in terms of 'where to play' and the back-end of the lifecycle in terms of 'how to scale'. Technologies such as robotic market intelligence will help managers to keep better tabs on emerging market trends and technologies, and simulation techniques and algorithms will help managers run 'what-if' scenarios for their world-building, digital futures.

At a turning point in the war, in November 1942, British Prime Minister Winston Churchill stated that

> Now this is not the end. It is not even the beginning of the end. But it is, perhaps, the end of the beginning.

This sentiment could not be more true for digital transformation. We're at the beginning of an exciting journey that will take us into the next ten years and beyond. While the term 'digital transformation' may change, you can be sure it will continue to be both 'digital' and a 'transformation.

APPENDIX
DIGITAL TRANSFORMATION MATURITY ASSESSMENT

The following set of assessment questions are intended to help you assess your organisation's current digital transformation maturity along each of the six dimensions that we outlined in Chapter 13, 'The agile journey to the new platform'. Please refer to this chapter for further information about the model. In terms of assessing and responding to your maturity level in each dimension, please see the section below entitled 'Assessing your maturity level'.

Question 1: Transformation objectives (strategy and vision) – With regard to your digital transformation objectives, please select the most appropriate response that describes your current strategy, focus and investments:

- Our transformation objectives are narrowly targeted in specific areas such as the digital workplace and improving operations **(Early)**.

- Our transformation objectives include re-thinking and re-designing our business processes as well as select initiatives related to the digital customer experience **(Developing)**.

- Our transformation objectives encompass re-thinking and re-designing our business models and processes and we are pursuing a mastery of the digital customer experience **(Maturing)**.

Question 2: Disruptive technologies (technology and capabilities) – With regard to your digital transformation initiatives, please select the most appropriate response that describes your current use of emerging and disruptive technologies:

- We routinely use SMAC technologies for our digital business applications **(Early)**.

- We routinely use SMAC technologies as well as select next-generation enablers (such as the IoT and intelligent automation) for our digital business applications **(Developing)**.

- We routinely use SMAC technologies as well as a strategic set of next-generation enablers (such as the IoT and intelligent automation) for our digital business applications **(Maturing)**.

Question 3: Platform business models (technology and capabilities) – With regard to your digital transformation strategy, please select the most appropriate response that describes your use of platform business models:

- We have no current use or plans for platform business models **(Early)**.
- We are actively investigating platform business models and their technical architectures **(Developing)**.
- Platform business models are already a core part of our digital transformation strategy **(Maturing)**.

Question 4: Digital services mastery (technology and capabilities) – With regard to how you design, develop, deploy, manage and continually evolve your digital services, please select the most appropriate response that describes your mastery of each of the six key capabilities (agile, DevOps, as-a-service infrastructure, intelligent automation, personas and context, and digital service management):

- We have a mastery of one or two of the key capabilities **(Early)**.
- We have a mastery of three or four of the key capabilities **(Developing)**.
- We have a mastery of five or six of the key capabilities **(Maturing)**.

Question 5: Organise for digital business innovation (process and governance) – With regard to your innovation management capability, please select the most appropriate response that describes your programme:

- We have limited and/or fragmented innovation programmes across the organisation **(Early)**.
- We have a formal enterprise-wide innovation programme, but have not yet tuned it for our digital transformation objectives **(Developing)**.
- We have a formal enterprise-wide innovation programme, which has been fine-tuned for our digital transformation objectives, and which enables continuous and collaborative innovation **(Maturing)**.

Question 6: Taking the agile journey to the future platform (people and culture) – With regard to your digital transformation journey, please select the most appropriate response that describes your current level of leadership, culture and digital skills:

- We have a risk averse culture and limited digital skills **(Early)**.
- We have a risk tolerant culture and moderate digital skills **(Developing)**.
- We have a risk receptive culture and strong digital skills **(Maturing)**.

Assessing your maturity level

Table A1 is intended to help assess your maturity level and provide some recommendations for how you can advance along each of the six dimensions outlined in Chapter 13, 'The agile journey to the new platform'.

Table A.1 Recommended actions based on results of your Digital Transformation Maturity Assessment

Digital transformation dimension	If you rated as 'Early'	If you rated as 'Developing'
Transformation objectives (strategy and vision)	• Review Chapters 1 and 2 (Re-thinking and re-designing business models and processes) • Review Chapter 8 (Strategic levers for the digital customer experience; the Digital Customer Experience Bill of Rights) • Review Chapters 9–11	• Review Chapters 1 and 2 (Re-thinking and re-designing business models) • Review Chapter 8 (the Digital Customer Experience Bill of Rights) • Review Chapters 9–11
Disruptive technologies (technology and capabilities)	• Review Chapter 3 (Beyond SMAC) • Review Chapter 4 (Exploiting the power of technology combinations) • Review Chapter 7 (Timing your move into disruptive technologies)	• Review Chapter 4 (Exploiting the power of technology combinations)
Platform business models (technology and capabilities)	• Review Chapter 4 (Exploiting the power of platform business models) • Review Chapter 7 (The three waves of disruptive technology adoption)	• Review Chapter 4 (Exploiting the power of platform business models)
Digital services mastery (technology and capabilities)	• Review Chapter 12 (Six key questions to ask of your current digital initiatives)	• Review Chapter 12 (Six key questions to ask of your current digital initiatives)

(continued)

Table A.1 (Continued)

Digital transformation dimension	If you rated as 'Early'	If you rated as 'Developing'
Organise for digital business innovation (process and governance)	• Review Chapter 5 (The five critical pillars of innovation management capability; Adapting innovation programmes for digital transformation) • Review Chapter 6 (Setting the rhythm of digital innovation: event based or ongoing ideation; Planning your Innovation Workshop)	• Review Chapter 5 (Adapting innovation programmes for digital transformation) • Review Chapter 6 (Setting the rhythm of digital innovation: event based or ongoing ideation)
Take the agile journey to the future platform (people and culture)	• Review Chapter 13	• Review Chapter 13

REFERENCES

CHAPTER 1

1. Andreessen, M. (2011) *Why software is eating the world. The Wall Street Journal.* Available from: www.wsj.com/articles/SB10001424053111903480904576512250 915629460 [7 November 2016].

2. Streetline (2016) Available from: www.streetline.com/smart-cities/infographic-smart-parking-at-a-glance/ [7 November 2016].

3. Porter, M.E. (1980) *Competitive strategy.* New York: Free Press.

4. Perry, Mark J. (2014) *Fortune 500 firms in 1955 vs 2014.* American Enterprise Institute. Available from: www.aei.org/publication/fortune-500-firms-in-1955-vs-2014-89-are-gone-and-were-all-better-off-because-of-that-dynamic-creative-destruction/ [7 November 2016].

5. Wang, R. 'Ray' (2016) *Dominate digital disruption before it dominates you.* Constellation Research. Available from: www.constellationr.com/users/r-ray-wang [7 November 2016].

6. Morozov, Evgeny (2015) *Where Uber and Amazon rule: welcome to the world of the platform. The Guardian.* Available from: www.theguardian.com/technology/2015/jun/07/facebook-uber-amazon-platform-economy [7 November 2016].

7. Tipping, A., Schmahl, A. and Duiven F. (2015) *Commercial transportation trends.* Strategy&. Available from: www.strategyand.pwc.com/perspectives/2015-commercial-transportation-trends [7 November 2016].

8. Johnson, E. (2015) *DHL tests wearable technology warehousing with Ricoh.* American Shipper. Available from: http://americanshipper.com/Main/News/DHL_tests_wearable_technology_warehousing_with_Ric_59325.aspx [7 November 2016].

CHAPTER 2

1. Christensen, C. (n.d.) BrainyQuote.com. Available from: www.brainyquote.com/quotes/quotes/c/claytonchr671437.html [7 November 2016].

2. Grothaus, M. (2016) *Apple Pay leads mobile payments with 12 million monthly users.* Fast Company. Available from: www.fastcompany.com/3057353/fast-feed/apple-pay-leads-mobile-payments-with-12-million-monthly-users [7 November 2016].

3. Hammer, M. and Champy, J. (1993) *Reengineering the corporation.* New York: Harper Business.

4. Airbnb (2016) Available from: www.airbnb.com/about/about-us [7 November 2016].

5. P&G (2016) Connect + Develop. Available from: www.pgconnectdevelop.com/ [7 November 2016].

6. Ross, P. (2016) *Tesla reveals its crowdsourced autopilot data.* IEEE Spectrum. Available from: http://spectrum.ieee.org/cars-that-think/transportation/self-driving/tesla-reveals-its-crowdsourced-autopilot-data [7 November 2016].

7. Earley, K. (2016) *Access over ownership is the future of consumption. The Guardian.* Available from: www.theguardian.com/sustainable-business/access-over-ownership-future-consumption [7 November 2016].

8. Zipcar (2016) Available from: www.zipcar.com/how#how-to-zip [7 November 2016].

9. Hamblen, M. (2015) *Apple Pay heads across the pond.* Computerworld. Available from: www.computerworld.com/article/2932608/retail-it/apple-pay-heads-across-the-pond.html [7 November 2016].

10. Apple (2014) *Apple announces Apple Pay.* Available from: www.apple.com/pr/library/2014/09/09Apple-Announces-Apple-Pay.html [7 November 2016].

11. Apple (2015) *Apple & China UnionPay to bring Apple Pay to China.* Available from: www.apple.com/pr/library/2015/12/18Apple-China-UnionPay-to-Bring-Apple-Pay-to-China.html [7 November 2016].

12. Vazquez Sampere, J.P. (2015) *Apple Pay is just a big giveaway to credit card companies. Harvard Business Review.* Available from: https://hbr.org/2015/04/apple-pay-is-just-a-big-giveaway-to-credit-card-companies [7 November 2016].

13. Parker, G., Van Alstyne, M. and Choudary, S. (2016) *Platform revolution.* New York: Norton.

14. Apple (2016) *United Airlines. Cleared for takeoff with iPad.* Available from: www.apple.com/ipad/business/profiles/united-airlines/ [7 November 2016].

15. Chase (2016) QuickDeposit. Available from: www.chase.com/online/digital/mobile-deposits.html [7 November 2016].

CHAPTER 3

1. Clarke, A. (n.d.) The Arthur C. Clarke Foundation. Available from: www.clarkefoundation.org/about-sir-arthur/sir-arthurs-quotations/ [7 November 2016].

2. Samuels, M. (n.d.) *Surviving disruption*. BCS Whitepaper. Available from: www.bcs.org/upload/pdf/surviving-disruption.pdf [7 November 2016].

3. Measey, P. (2015) *Agile foundations – principles, practices and frameworks*. British Computer Society. Available from: http://shop.bcs.org/display.asp?k=9781780172545 [7 November 2016].

4. Gartner (2016) *DevOps*. Gartner IT Glossary. Available from: http://blogs.gartner.com/it-glossary/devops/ [7 November 2016].

5. Uber (2015) *What to expect when you ride*. Available from: https://newsroom.uber.com/uber-safety-transparency/ [7 November 2016].

6. GOV.UK (2016) *About the Government Digital Service*. Available from: https://gds.blog.gov.uk/about/ [7 November 2016].

7. Foreshew-Cain, S. (2015) *How digital and technology transformation saved £1.7bn last year*. Government Digital Service. Available from: https://gds.blog.gov.uk/2015/10/23/how-digital-and-technology-transformation-saved-1-7bn-last-year/ [7 November 2016].

8. Foreshew-Cain, S. (2016) Personal interview.

9. Downe, L. (2015) *Better services with patterns and standards*. Government Digital Service. Available from: https://gds.blog.gov.uk/2015/08/06/better-services-with-patterns-and-standards/ [7 November 2016].

10. GOV.UK (2016) *Services data*. Available from: https://www.gov.uk/performance/services [7 November 2016].

11. Downey, P. (2015) *Registers: authoritative lists you can trust*. Government Digital Service. Available from: https://gds.blog.gov.uk/2015/09/01/registers-authoritative-lists-you-can-trust/ [7 November 2016].

12. Foreshew-Cain, S. (2016) *Where we're at, and where we're going*. Government Digital Service. Available from: https://gds.blog.gov.uk/2016/04/08/where-were-at-and-where-were-going/ [7 November 2016].

13. Foreshew-Cain, S. (2016) *Where we're at, and where we're going*. Government Digital Service. Available from: https://gds.blog.gov.uk/2016/04/08/where-were-at-and-where-were-going/ [7 November 2016].

CHAPTER 4

1. Evans, P. and Gawyer, A. (2016) *The rise of the platform enterprise: a global survey.* The Center for Global Enterprise. Available from: http://thecge.net/archived-papers/the-rise-of-the-platform-enterprise-a-global-survey/ [7 November 2016].

2. GE (2012) *Industrial Internet: pushing the boundaries of minds and machines.* Available from: www.ge.com/docs/chapters/Industrial_Internet.pdf [7 November 2016].

3. IDC (2015) *IDC expands research coverage for six key innovation accelerators.* Available from: www.idc.com/getdoc.jsp?containerId=prUS25991715 [7 November 2016].

4. Progressive Insurance (2016) *Snapshot.* Available from: www.progressive.com/auto/snapshot/ [7 November 2016].

5. Ring™ (2016) Available from: www.ring.com [7 November 2016].

6. Mayor of London (2015) *Mayor on track to roll-out police body cameras across the Met.* Available from: www.london.gov.uk/press-releases/mayoral/mayor-on-track-to-roll-out-police-body-cameras [7 November 2016].

7. Johnson, E. (2015) *DHL tests wearable technology warehousing with Ricoh.* American Shipper. Available from: http://americanshipper.com/Main/News/DHL_tests_wearable_technology_warehousing_with_Ric_59325.aspx [7 November 2016].

8. Accenture (2016) *Accenture technology vision 2016. Platform economy.* Available from: www.accenture.com/us-en/insight-digital-platform-economy [7 November 2016].

9. GE (2016) *Predix platform overview.* Available from: www.ge.com/digital/predix [7 November 2016].

10. GE Platform Brief (2016) *Predix: the platform for the Industrial Internet.* Platform brief. Available from: www.ge.com/digital/sites/default/files/Predix-the-platform-for-the-Industrial-Internet-whitepaper.pdf [7 November 2016].

11. Parker, G., Van Alstyne, M. and Choudary, S. (2016) *Platform revolution.* New York: Norton.

12. *Wall Street Journal* (2015) *Airbnb raises $1.5 billion in one of the largest private placements.* Available from: www.wsj.com/articles/airbnb-raises-1-5-billion-in-one-of-largest-private-placements-1435363506 [7 November 2016].

13. RAC (2016) *RAC acquires Nebula Systems to boost power of telematics.* Available from: www.rac.co.uk/press-centre#/pressreleases/rac-acquires-nebula-systems-to-boost-power-of-telematics-1330291 [7 November 2016].

14. Welborn, Ralph (2016) Imaginatik, Personal interview.

15. IDC (2015) *IDC predicts the emergence of 'the DX economy' in a critical period of widespread digital transformation and massive scale up of 3rd platform technologies in every industry*. Press release. Available from: www.idc.com/getdoc. jsp?containerId=prUS40552015 [7 November 2016].

16. Federal Ministry of Education and Research (2013) *Recommendations for implementing the strategic initiative INDUSTRIE 4.0*. Available from: www.acatech. de/fileadmin/user_upload/Baumstruktur_nach_Website/Acatech/root/de/ Material_fuer_Sonderseiten/Industrie_4.0/Final_report__Industrie_4.0_accessible. pdf [7 November 2016].

17. PwC (2016) *Industry 4.0 offers industry players the potential for high growth and improved efficiency*. Available from: www.pwc.de/en/digitale-transformation/pwc-studie-industrie-4-0-steht-vor-dem-durchbruch.html [7 November 2016].

18. Industrial Internet Consortium (2016) Available from: www.iiconsortium.org/ [7 November 2016].

CHAPTER 5

1. Jobs, S. (n.d.) BrainyQuote.com. Available from: www.brainyquote.com/quotes/ quotes/s/stevejobs173474.html [7 November 2016].

2. Sanders, David (2015) Dallas Advisory Partners, Personal interview.

3. Corporate Executive Board (2016) Available from: www.cebglobal.com/ [7 November 2016].

4. P&G (2016) *Connect + Develop*. Available from: www.pgconnectdevelop.com/ [7 November 2016].

5. Hill, Steven (2015) KPMG, Personal interview.

6. Welborn, Ralph (2015) Imaginatik, Personal interview.

7. Baghai, M., Coley, S. and White, D. (2000) *The alchemy of growth*. New York: Basic Books.

8. Hill, Steven (2015) KPMG, Personal interview.

9. Christensen, C. (1997) *The innovator's dilemma*. Brighton, MA: Harvard Business Review Press.

CHAPTER 6

1. Gates, B. (2007) *The skills you need to succeed*. Available from: http://news.bbc. co.uk/2/hi/business/7142073.stm [7 November 2016]

2. PwC. (2015) 18th CEO Survey 2015. Available from: www.pwc.com/gx/en/ceo-agenda/ceosurvey/2015/key-findings/technology.html [7 November 2016].

CHAPTER 7

1. Musashi, M. (n.d.) BrainyQuote.com. Available from: www.brainyquote.com/quotes/quotes/m/miyamotomu135552.html [7 November 2016].

2. Wikipedia (2016) Technology adoption life cycle. Available from: http://en.wikipedia.org/wiki/Technology_adoption_lifecycle [24 November 2016].

3. *MIT Technology Review* (2012) *Mobile computing in question*. Available from: www.technologyreview.com/news/427787/are-smart-phones-spreading-faster-than-any/ [7 November 2016].

4. Wikipedia (2016) *Color television*. Available from: https://en.wikipedia.org/wiki/Color_television#Adoption [7 November 2016].

5. GOV.UK (2016) *Digital by default service standard*. Available from: www.gov.uk/service-manual/digital-by-default [7 November 2016].

6. Whitehouse.Gov (2012) *Digital government: building a 21st century platform to better serve the American people*. Available from: www.whitehouse.gov/sites/default/files/omb/egov/digital-government/digital-government-strategy.pdf [7 November 2016].

7. McKinsey Global Institute (2012) *The social economy: unlocking value and productivity through social technologies*. Available from: www.mckinsey.com/industries/high-tech/our-insights/the-social-economy [7 November 2016].

CHAPTER 8

1. Bezos, J. (2004) *Online extra: Jeff Bezos on word-of-mouth power*. Bloomberg. Available from: www.bloomberg.com/news/articles/2004-08-01/online-extra-jeff-bezos-on-word-of-mouth-power [7 November 2016].

2. Ring™ (2016) Available from: www.ring.com [7 November 2016].

3. Walt Disney World (2016) *My Disney experience – frequently asked questions*. Available from: https://disneyworld.disney.go.com/faq/my-disney-experience/frequency-technology/ [7 November 2016].

4. Savioke (2016) *Beyond hospitality: how robots can improve your customer experience anywhere*. Available from: www.savioke.com/blog/2016/6/15/beyond-hospitality-how-robots-can-improve-your-customer-experience-anywhere [7 November 2016].

5. Rajesh, M. (2015) *Inside Japan's first robot-staffed hotel*. *The Guardian*. Available from: www.theguardian.com/travel/2015/aug/14/japan-henn-na-hotel-staffed-by-robots [7 November 2016].

6. American Airlines (2016) *American Airlines app*. Available from: www.aa.com/i18n/ travel-info/travel-tools/american-airlines-app.jsp [7 November 2016].

7. Millward, D. (2013) *Drivers to be banned from wearing Google Glass. The Telegraph*. Available from: www.telegraph.co.uk/technology/news/10214822/Drivers-to-be-banned-from-wearing-Google-Glass.html [7 November 2016].

CHAPTER 9

1. Brooks, R. (2010) *The robot invasion is coming – and that's a good thing*. Discover. Available from: http://discovermagazine.com/2010/oct/13-rodney-brooks-robot-invasion [7 November 2016].

2. Davenport, T. and Kirby, J. (2015) *Beyond automation. Harvard Business Review*. Available from: https://hbr.org/2015/06/beyond-automation [7 November 2016].

3. Knight, W. (2015) *A transformer wins DARPA's $2 million robotics challenge. MIT Technology Review*. Available from https://www.technologyreview.com/s/538136/ a-transformer-wins-darpas-2-million-robotics-challenge/ [7 November 2016].

4. Amazon (2016) *Amazon and UK Government aim for the sky with partnership on drones*. Press release. Available from: http://phx.corporate-ir.net/phoenix. zhtml?c=176060&p=irol-newsArticle&ID=2188074 [7 November 2016].

5. Amazon (2016) *Amazon and UK Government aim for the sky with partnership on drones*. Press release. Available from: http://phx.corporate-ir.net/phoenix. zhtml?c=176060&p=irol-newsArticle&ID=2188074 [7 November 2016].

CHAPTER 10

1. Sondergaard, P. (2011) *Gartner*. Press release. Available from: www.gartner.com/ newsroom/id/1824919 [7 November 2016].

2. IDC (2016) *FutureScape: worldwide big data and analytics 2016 predictions*. Available from: www.cloudera.com/content/dam/www/static/documents/analyst-reports/ idc-futurescape.pdf [7 November 2016].

3. EMC (2014) *Digital universe invaded by sensors*. Press release. Available from: www. emc.com/about/news/press/2014/20140409-01.htm [7 November 2016].

4. IBM (n.d.) *The four V's of big data*. Available from: www.ibmbigdatahub.com/ infographic/four-vs-big-data [7 November 2016].

5. IBM (n.d.) *The four V's of big data*. Available from: www.ibmbigdatahub.com/ infographic/four-vs-big-data [7 November 2016].

6. Domo (2016) *Data never sleeps 4.0*. Available from: www.domo.com/blog/2016/06/data-never-sleeps-4-0/ [7 November 2016].

7. Cloudera (2016) *Siemens PLM software's enterprise data hub helps manufacturers save millions*. Available from: www.cloudera.com/customers/siemens.html [7 November 2016].

8. Thibodeau, P. (2013) *Data that's here today could be gone tomorrow, says Cerf*. Computerworld. Available from: www.computerworld.com/article/2497802/enterprise-applications/data-that-s-here-today-could-be-gone-tomorrow--says-cerf.html [7 November 2016].

9. Southampton University (2016) *Eternal 5D data storage could record the history of humankind*. Available from: www.southampton.ac.uk/news/2016/02/5d-data-storage-update.page [7 November 2016].

10. Vincent, J. (2016) *Five-dimensional glass discs can store data for up to 13.8 billion years*. The Verge. Available from: www.theverge.com/2016/2/16/11018018/5d-data-storage-glass [7 November 2016].

11. P&G (2016) *Business sphere fact sheet*. Available from: www.pg.com/en_US/downloads/innovation/factsheet_BusinessSphere.pdf [7 November 2016].

CHAPTER 11

1. Schwab, K. (2015) *Are you ready for the technological revolution?* World Economic Forum. Available from: www.weforum.org/agenda/2015/02/are-you-ready-for-the-technological-revolution/ [7 November 2016].

2. British Continuity Institute (2016) *Cyber attack top business threat for second year running*. Press release. Available from: www.thebci.org/index.php/about/news-room#/pressreleases/cyber-attack-top-business-threat-for-second-year-running-1310591 [7 November 2016].

3. Gartner (2015) *Forecast: public cloud service brokerage, 4Q14*. Available from: www.gartner.com/doc/2985118/forecast-public-cloud-service-brokerage [7 November 2016].

4. Gartner (2013) *Top 10 strategic technology trends for 2014*. Symposium ITxpo. Press release. Available from: www.gartner.com/newsroom/id/2603623 [7 November 2016].

5. TechTarget (2016) *ITSM definition*. Available from: http://searchitoperations.techtarget.com/definition/ITSM [7 November 2016].

6. Drinkwater, D. (2014) *RSA 2014: CISOs must move beyond perimeter-based security*. SC Magazine. Available from: www.scmagazine.com/rsa-2014-cisos-must-move-beyond-perimeter-based-security/article/538201/ [7 November 2016].

7.   Gartner (2013) *Predicts 2014: infrastructure protection*. Gartner report. Available from: www.gartner.com/doc/2629230/predicts--infrastructure-protection [7 November 2016].

8.   World Economic Forum (2014) *Risk and responsibility in a hyperconnected world*. Available from: www3.weforum.org/docs/WEF_RiskResponsibility_HyperconnectedWorld_Report_2014.pdf [7 November 2016].

9.   eWeek (2015) *Micro-segmentation: a better way to defend the data center*. Available from: www.eweek.com/security/slideshows/micro-segmentation-a-better-way-to-defend-the-data-center.html [7 November 2016].

CHAPTER 12

1.   Benioff, Marc R. (2016) *36 best quotes from Davos 2016*. Available from: www.weforum.org/agenda/2016/01/36-best-quotes-of-davos-2016/ [7 November 2016].

2.   CIA (2016) *The world factbook*. Available from: www.cia.gov/library/publications/the-world-factbook/geos/xx.html [7 November 2016].

3.   McKinsey (2015) *Service innovation in a digital world*. Available from: www.mckinsey.com/business-functions/operations/our-insights/service-innovation-in-a-digital-world [7 November 2016].

4.   McKinsey (2014) *Why companies should care about e-care*. Available from: www.mckinsey.com/business-functions/marketing-and-sales/our-insights/why-companies-should-care-about-ecare [7 November 2016].

5.   Gartner (2016) *Gartner reveals top predictions for IT organizations and users for 2015 and beyond*. Press release. Available from: www.gartner.com/newsroom/id/2866617 [7 November 2016].

CHAPTER 13

1.   Darwin, C. (n.d.) *On the origin of species*. Available from: http://quoteinvestigator.com/2014/05/04/adapt/ [7 November 2016].

CONCLUSION

1.   Churchill, W. (1942) *The end of the beginning*. The Churchill Society. Available from: www.churchill-society-london.org.uk/EndoBegn.html [7 November 2016].

2.   Global Center for Digital Business Transformation (2015) *Digital vortex*. Available from: www.imd.org/uupload/IMD.WebSite/DBT/Digital_Vortex_06182015.pdf [7 November 2016].

INDEX

Lightning Source UK Ltd.
Milton Keynes UK
UKHW031526220621
385966UK00006B/97